Praise for *The Alphabet of Aliens*

"Sabyasachi Nag's new, unique prose poetry gives us the truth, pain, and mad splendor of the 'alien'. *The Alphabet of Aliens* is a cascade of brilliant surreal stories braided with moments of condensed lyricism and concentrated, brutal yet witty, recognition. Nag has created a style that delivers the oft-proclaimed but rarely embraced and expressed fact that the alien is not only a foreigner, an extraterrestrial, but is a symbol, an inner reality, of each of us. What 'alienation' is and what it makes us see, within and around us, is revealed again and again in brilliant poems and their brilliant images, insights, and phrases. Their brilliant music. *The Alphabet of Aliens* is a book of a marvelous and disturbing experience, of a self's remorseless, exploratory descent into difficult reality, into 'a soundless tree-cave reflecting a trapped sun. And there we stop and realize we are not yet dead; we are here, still breathing.'"

—A F MORITZ, author of *Great Silent Ballad*

"Sabyasachi Nag's *The Alphabet of Aliens* opens with the line 'As an alien you are entitled to nothing,' but this collection of electric prose poems is full to bursting with ants, blood, tea, winter, dragons, tornadoes, mothers, fathers, lions, crows, beetles. He stops at the Insomnia Motel, The Curry Shop, boards the Spice Train looking for his place in the world. 'I was a dream,' he says. 'Dreams are wishes.' Oh, the dreams that come cascading through the pages of this generous book. There are wonders on every page and crazy delight."

—BARBARA HAMBY, author of *Burn*

"*The Alphabet of Aliens*, prose poems by Sabyasachi Nag, is quite simply, superb. Nag's words teleport, transmute, and inject the reader into the emotional psyche of anyone, everyone, who's ever been an outsider. This is the work of an astute writer. Evoking emotions I suspect we all share and more often than not, try to ignore, or to bury. Both polished and raw, each piece reminds me of a sophisticated, deconstructed meal prepared by a master chef. One who knows better than anyone what works, and how best to present that to showcase judiciously chosen ingredients. This is a book I will reread, and benefit from every time. Kudos to Mawenzi House, and hats off to Sabyasachi Nag. *The Alphabet of Aliens* is a gift to us all."

—BILL ARNOTT, author of *A Perfect Day for a Walk* and *A Perfect Day for a Walk by the Water*

"Cold and hot at the same time, *The Alphabet of Aliens* pushes the reader away and pulls the reader in—forcing uncomfortable intimacy with the old, old learning curve of newness that attends the migrant experience. The phonetic is frenetic in Nag's worlds within words. It's playful, and it's painful."

—CHANTEL LAVOIE, author of *This Is About Angels, Women, and Men*

"*The Alphabet of Aliens* is a triumph: Songs cast in ecstatic surrealism: You're betwixt 'Strawberry Fields' and 'Desolation Row,' in that space where Rilke meets Ferlinghetti. And once there, you won't want to leave. Promise! Lookit! 'Last night screams from the epidemic filled the arteries of the harmonica . . . Let's not say another word. Not today. There's enough already said in the libraries of the world.'"

—GEORGE ELLIOTT CLARKE, author of *Canticles I-II-III (MMXVI-MMXXIII)*

"No gossamer romance, *The Alphabet of Aliens* often sings against a sky stooping down like a heavy song itself. Often eerie, this collection of prose poems investigates the nature, scope, and meaning of migrancy. Part diary, part dream book, it is a long, winding meditation on worlds lost and recovered. As images hurtle at us, we discover how the past keeps invading us while we go about seeking truth as surely as bees and ants seek sugar. Its huge arc of engaging, conflicting, perplexing impressions and reflections creates stunning metamorphoses in a scrambled rhythm. Stuffed with kaleidoscopic scenes from life and dream, it is an extravagant experiment, as if Kafka were refracted through Dali."

—KEITH GAREBIAN, theatre scholar, literary critic, and poet

"The beauty and whimsy of *The Alphabet of Aliens* will pull you into its text; once you're immersed in this startling and compelling book of poems, the words will get their hooks into your heart and not let go."

—RHEA TREGEBOV, author of *Talking to Strangers*

"Nag's tight prose along and his interweaving of nature's beautiful images and unique voices throughout this collection captures the narrator's dilemma and makes the reader feel these experiences. Well done. Nag is a master of his craft."

—STELLA LEVENTOYANNIS HARVEY, author of *Finding Callidora*

"Sabyasachi Nag's *The Alphabet of Aliens* is a triumph of vision, writing, and sustained expression of its subject. Nag's writing reminds the reader of other great writers of outsider literature, for instance Kafka, Orwell, and even William Burroughs."

—STEPHEN MORRISSEY, author of *Farewell, Darkness: Selected poems*

THE ALPHABET OF ALIENS

prose poems

sabyasachi nag

MAWENZI
HOUSE

We acknowledge the support of the Canada Council for the Arts for our publishing program. We also acknowledge support from the Government of Ontario through the Ontario Arts Council, and the support of the Government of Canada through the Canada Book Fund.

Cover art: tttuna / Clouds and stars paper cutting style stock photo/ iStockphoto
Cover design by Kay Dee En and Sabrina Pignataro

Library and Archives Canada Cataloguing in Publication

Title: The alphabet of aliens : poetry / Sabyasachi Nag.

Names: Nag, Sabyasachi, 1968- author.

Identifiers: Canadiana (print) 20250260506 | Canadiana (ebook) 20250260522 | ISBN 9781774152010 (softcover) | ISBN 9781774152027 (EPUB) | ISBN 9781774152034 (PDF)

Subjects: LCGFT: Poetry.

Classification: LCC PS8627.A483 A79 2025 | DDC C811/.6—dc23

Printed and bound in Canada by Coach House Printing

Mawenzi House Publishers Ltd
192 Spadina Ave, Suite 417
Toronto, ON, M5T 2C2
Canada

www.mawenzihouse.com

For My Mother

CONTENTS

As an Alien, You Are Entitled

As an alien, you are entitled to nothing. But, since no one can be nothing for long, you chance your way to the prospect park—an electric grill to boil your potato—a hammer to nail your headshot. No longer incognito, you find out you are not the only one in your head—echoes from the past have followed you. And since you have paid them the uncommon rent, when you bring this anomalous tinnitus to their attention, the authorities start probing you for treason: *wtf are you cooking inside*? But you are sure, you are not the only one. This rogue ringing your head crawls mysteriously in and out cracks in the baseboard, damages the crown rails dragging his trolley overflowing with old clothes, dog-eared books, rubbish cans containing rocks scavenged from fallen stars. He has a distinct odour. And in his thick accent, rambles off-key into the rutty cornet. Sometimes he pulls out a broken accordion and belts out old country songs or writes illegibly on a chalkboard. You tolerate him. Then he starts eating up the lilac and amaryllis, starts skinning the songbirds, leaves a trail of his waste everywhere. Even though he evokes lush memories and romantic escapades there's no way you are going to put up with that. You spend the night waiting for him to fall asleep so you can throttle him. Guess what? The rascal sleeps all day, operates at night, from a faraway place impossible to reach eyes open. And since you and he occupy the same hollow in the brain's hippocampus, smothering him while he's asleep would be, in a way, suicidal. Friendship is impossible because you have only just escaped him. His clothes are smoked in the sulphur of scabs you are trying to forget. How to get rid of the intruder? You haven't a clue. You couldn't inject poison into his lungs or visit a surgeon to have him extracted because the X-rays reveal nothing. You can't ignore him either. You can't stop being in the funk, can't gather yourself. *Who are you?* You finally face up, one lazy afternoon. He's startled. *Who are you,* he hits back with a flyswatter, his voice like your own pipsqueak from grade school. You laugh. You weep. You have no choice.

The Alphabet of Aliens

A for apple, B for blow-in. Aliens love them. Everyone knows it. But when the boy comes home he chews on his blood. When the girl comes home she chews on her case. And deaths come dressed like deferred action, deportation. E for education; F for family, G for government action, inaction, requital, retribution. The homeless move like a shadow infantry minus horses. And when they come invading, they act like ants. Because ants crave sugar. Ants make sugar. Ants can't do without an alphabet that has no apple sugar. The boy says he's the ant with a joy jug in his head, the owl with a sugar heart, the parrot with a sugar tongue made from cochineal bugs. The boy builds tunnels. The boy loves fables. The girl pulls her red tongue to the mirror. She makes chances with the make-do name; makes dates in make-do calendars. In a country of chained migration, her alphabet has no letters; wax walls made of here, elsewhere, soul, freedom. He loves being waivered. She hates being X-rayed. It's hard to skin him, harder still to parse her yak-belly alpha beta theta. Not the usual twenty-six. Not the zigzagged zebra of merit and quota. I know my hunger. Speaks in multiple tongues—appeal, affidavit, asylum, amnesty, adjustment of status. Aliens are for apples. Apples at the start, in the middle, and at the end. Apples for all seasons, apples in every grocery aisle, apples in every drug store. Sweetness spiked in sin. Apples, for centuries, since Eden.

The Alien Fear

Having escaped their fate in the parliament of punks the alien is scared of the heart's inevitable collapse. When they enter a field of corn, cut in halves by the alien green, angled toward the horse hooves in the alien sky, they fear they will supplant ancient chants of elsewhere with anthems of crickets here, shadowing the gold tassels dancing the wind. When they tutor the child with deep philosophies of the aspen and pine, they fear they'll lose the songs of origin that healed their wounds. And in the heat of their humiliations, they cook their poppies. When they dig the cold ground to bury the dead, they fear they'll forget their debts. Before they offer their final word for the bull-headed children, all set to scatter around alien oceans, they ask for time, because they don't want to be lonely again, because their loneliness has no limits, because their ruin is the only one they remember, because their dreams look like calluses on empty hands, because the creases crossing eyes have cracked the mirror, because their history burned a hole into the heart and the blue morning is like turned milk and hurt is the only resting place until afternoon. The alien fears new bridges in the offing after old walls have fallen. In the pothole of rotten rain, the alien is anxious they'll be asked to puncture their own belly and aspire the blood, because they need work, and they remember ancestors who were asked to build walls with bricks from broken bridges.

Grammar for New Arrivals

Shortly after I landed someone said, go cook it. So, I went to a convenience store to get my game on—asked for napkins so I could scribble down cram notes: how to caulk eyes, winterize the tongue, insulate lips, weather strip lungs, install new storm windows. It's a different matter nothing works in the face of the freeze pop. A boy coins the laundry, a girl colours her nails red and white, a man hangs on static outside a glass facade, a woman on a knife-point blinks behind a curtained cubicle. And it's a whole new dictionary of Molson muscles, beavertail and butter tart. To make sense of poutine and Tortière without a toque, ooh! So much easier in the elsewhere of watercress where you just turn the keys with star anise in the teas, where the deep well is lighted with crushed moonstones and the fork in the tongue is quilted in cardamom. *Why then does anyone leave?* The officer nodded when I looked past the candy cane. It was nearly Christmas. And, as I fished for my keys to the spice trunk she chuckled *you don't have to answer.* And when I boarded the transit and started ripping the duct tape off my heart, someone said *don't look at him.* And when I wandered the streets around needles and caution tape or took the ropeways to the crystal peaks high up the lag-gravel, quickly arriving nouns sparkled briefly, before they broke down like pappus. Someone said, *to get on the Bumbleberry pie you need to requalify*. So, what, if new verbs were new labours, new forests were new prepositions of arrival and silence the new interjection? A primal urge drove me to the conjugate of ice and libido, under the blinking window I became the silhouette: ladybug on the chin, ant on the sea of Yin, eyes wide open. But the sun, like clingy sugar, stood a wall of blinds. For a long shot, I wanted to be the knife, the mis en scene. For a long time, I wanted to do nothing but train my tongue, sew the snake-fork, stitched into this new grammar.

At the Zoo on Monday

At the zoo on Monday, no matter how many times I try my hand at *What Animal Are You* I am always the sugar ant—the single-minded super-organism—architect of invisible megalopolises conjoined underground like a super colony spanning continents, centuries, colour charts. I am the inverted creation story, a flight of spiral stairs off the main street down to the bottomless pit, minutes before redemption. Even though I've been busy moving earth through millennia—billions of ant loads, night after night, fifty times my body weight—no one knows about me but anthropologists, cosmologists, ethnologists and the police who have been studying my behaviour, the architecture of my underground. They dig holes all night, pour concrete into plastic tubes, employ mechanical diggers to excavate my history. They say they are studying the composition of my roots when in reality they are studying the fetor of my armpits. It's futile. Because being a sugar ant is not about want or character, it's about wounds you wear to the outhouse and gouge in the shower. And no one needs diggers to excavate wounds—tepid like a clouded star, toeing an invisible line on reflex, in obedience to the pull of that mammoth trigger, ever ready to get on with gravity, down the shaft off the main street to the dumpster, minutes before redemption. And since I'm hurtling down at speed my angst must be heavy, you think. And since I'm hurting in the head my wound must have to do with memory: how often have I been colonized and decolonized. But falling is a habit and I have fallen before. And winds don't bother me because I have been blown before. And wants don't bother me because I doubt they want me at all. And doubts don't bother me because no one can get rid of doubts. And truth doesn't bother me either. Many have tried to get to it. Drilled deeper holes. Sunk longer tubes. Poured more viscid concrete. Excavated ant colonies for centuries. Sealed entry points, laid the trap low during the day and at night, sugared the poisoned floor. It's futile. Ants have built roads underground not for nothing. Garbage dumps, fungus gardens, roundabouts; tunnels and turning points like the great wall of Shambhala—city of trapped light. I can walk on it; stop where I want. Everyone knows it exists, they have heard about it, but can't get there, because to reach that far you need to be ultra-light, almost hollow inside.

Briefly 'Bout Blood

Dust, wind, river, rock, sky, water should be among my beloved words—because I paid a price already—but I often brood about other words like bird-call, bird-seed, bannock, before I am distracted by blood, even though we see it everywhere, no one wants to talk about it and that's unfair because the blōd sound—the telling acoustic impact of the closed long vowel—can quickly spin a gossamer romance unless while chasing a bird in the backwoods you crash into a ditch in the dark set winter and limbs badly frozen you're banished to the story of that Chinese farmer who couldn't tell the difference between good news and bad; yet stories about blood are usually good news because they often come around Easter—but sometimes blood stories can be bad news if they are from distant places typical of Kafka, setting low expectations at the beginning before everyone is turned into a bug, and bug stories can be bizarre—much more than the one about the boy who met the beauty in the bodega and was bagged away by monsters—not believable monsters cloaked in business casuals—but real Brobdingnagians from outer space equipped with blunt tools that make shallow holes—so the boy who met the girl—or the girl who met the boy—can get out of bad news without a whole lot of blood—and that kind of blood is okay to bring up in polite conversations because it tastes like tomato sauce and foreshadows bottomless bliss before the after.

On the Art of Tea

It's only when you fail you worry about the way of things. She says, wait for the water to tell you it's ready. To take the leaves out of the bottle bubbles must move like an electric eel and the damp air must steal the flavour from the spoon.

Outside it's raining, a window is open. The shear has taken the shape of the smoke bush. A starling hangs the night on a clothesline and geraniums act like mothers in emptied nests. It hasn't fully dawned yet.

But the neighbour's cat is back in our yard nuzzling against the glass, amazed at his own shadow. He knows something else about the night, a sentience, beyond steel, water and fire, as if time were built into its nature, instinct.

The tea settles. The leaves open. Faces like anguished lovers looking for veins to split open. No, today no one would die for nothing. But to love is to suffer. All about the timing. No, she says. It's blood that stirs the shadow in the pot.

Winter at the Bardo

Again, it was winter. At the *Bardo,* they needed someone to crew lines where new aliens called toll-free to record their testimonies. *Nights of December, January, February and March are busy. What do you know about half-landings? How do you console someone scared of dead centres?*

With opiates and delirium, I said, *because the glut of sugar-glazed words has gutted dictionaries of their worth.* Then, I turned on the charm. It was hard to hear my own tongues, and I couldn't believe it when they called again to ask: *Can you wake up nights? Of course*, I was already having trouble holding my head to the pillow. Not for the lack of gravity, or posttraumatic nightmares from old-fashioned wars. Truth is, as an alien of no substance, I was hungry.

My little office in a remote corner by the boiler had bolted windows, a chair and a corded phone screwed to a stand. And they were kind—fed me crumb cakes, paid me on time, found me a bed vacated by someone who had suddenly vanished. First, it was her centre, then the peripheries, finally what remained was just the funk and frosted sugar—no one was certain she even existed.

Not completely invisible. Not to those who could see through the dark night, read the Bear Claw, she wheeled about like a remotely piloted apple fritter. And as I followed her, she traipsed between burnt balsam fir, black-backed pecker and owl, borers and beetle—pausing to watch frost patterns on scrub oak, chamise and manzanita, pergolas of circus spiders—under the spell of an invisible Sisyphus—for hours without word—an abyss staring an abyss—listening to the coyotes—seeking something—purpose, escape, afterlife—before being thrown down first by the wind, then by gravity.

We ate quietly. And now I felt pity. Before she started growing on me, like mildew, like morel, I found myself carving my own skin, putting her in my salads, loving the ease of the knife into her jelly heart birthing creamy wraiths. For a while, I became certain I was there to stand for her—carved a hole in the centre to let her settle in. And the idea of a donut locked in a donut kept me from holding my head to the pillow, a confused kind of love, as we never touched or talked.

From a distance it was clear there was a pattern to her trajectory—up to the nook by the weeping willows—dressed in dark vestal shadow like a prioress—she'd clear with bare hands frozen headstones between centuries-old charred white cedar and Douglas fir dunked in snow, before sliding downhill pulled by invisible djinns—her coat hemmed with mourning gems and spectral clocks—it was her passion for filling up the hollowed centre that had me grovelling, or maybe it was the gravity of her peculiar darkness, curly black hair bundled like an orchard of wood apples humming with bees, her shadow rotating an imaginary axial.

Each time I saw her—the fuzz on her tongue, funk of her ghosted pits, the raw rhytids of her ghosted mouth—I wanted to drink off her virgin rivers and I found a way to slide into her coiled apiary. Of course, it was locked and guarded. Of course, there were other bees inside her ten thousand heads. Of course, they swilled with long-bladed knives. And as I touched her, she began to weep.

We walked up the ghost hill—shadow-locked—and for once as we stood before the charred headstones, a murmur seemed to rise from the snowed field, form into a dirty-white patch-quilt of dense tree voice wrapped around our cold bodies—and when I reached for her mouth and poured into her the entirety of my truth and all the delusions tripped by mushrooms and dog-eared dictionaries—she went dead for a moment, before bloating like a ghastly pumpkin ready to be re-carved. I asked if I should restore her back to the state I found her. She shook her head, reached into her chest and lit a fire.

Fitting Dragons

Unlike other places where they make you strip before throwing you into a steamy cauldron, here they send you to the stone mason who ignores you for half a century before handing a square tassel to cut yourself into the scene. But since the slot is far from square you are then asked to visit the shed down the street where a one-eyed overseer supplies the tools to smooth edges, peel the debris off your tongue. And if you are cut up shorter than the allotted spit, they don't care; you adjust to expectations. Regular pennies made from square tiles fit anywhere. And if somehow you land up odder than stock standard, it's not that scandalous, just a couple more years in the corner room. But what if you are the ghost inhabiting a moon-eating dragon—a beast with three horns and mirror scales—impermeable to common weapons—immune to enhancement drugs? How do you deal with that? You wander the wild; hold your tongue; keep mouth open; wait for your poison. And when rain does arrive, you lean over the window and yell at the starry night. You search the stacked scrolls, repeat incessantly: *dragons are bird shadows in the Plato pad*. And when that doesn't work, you hope the dragons shift shape, take on the hairy head and body of your ancient youth. And if you still can't fit into the square scene in a square room, you fit into a square poem.

Rooms for Aliens

When the city ran out of art, the aldermen allowed windows painted into basements. The wind herded us, those from elsewhere, down to the crypt. But, as many of us in our family of doppelgangers look like old maple leaves, used tabloids and worn-out clothes, it was easy to have us stacked in drawers, clipped to hangers or folded inside Nordic chambers of perfectly quartered closets from Ikea. No one complained. Worming tight into the tulle and taffeta of Victoria's Secrets was in many ways a dream come true. Some of us who were hungry, occupied the lower drawers in the pantry, and in a fit of adrenaline, someone burst open a can of custard and meta morphed into a mantis before he could be captured and immediately quarantined. Our rooms were ant rooms, our hills were ant hills, our colonies ant colonies like the ones in Brazil, visible from outer space, the wainscotting loaded with replicas of colonial artifacts from ethno-nationalistic suites in marbled museums around the metaverse. Someone stuck up photos of ancient kings in the moulding framed in upcycled Africa and lined the picture rails with photos of ancient consorts in various postures of pleasure and lined the breadboards with grindstones. Then they hung upside down from the crown moulding capturing scenes from the kitchen and bathroom, temple and living room for dealers in alien art, auctioneers and connoisseurs of lost histories who took it all in and hung our rooms upside down, so we looked straight, in alignment with the weeping willows, loon in the moon and exploding sassafras.

The Long Night We Landed

The long night we landed we listened to the cicadas mistaking them for crickets. In complete submission—everything seemed perfect—the kind of listening that dissolves doubt about borders, limits—like that day my father died, and I realized, in the last stage of man there is no man, just a bag of unspeakable words. The sky stoops down like a heavy song. Takes it all. A single mound of cloud in the darkened sky moulded like a face. In a flash, he was gone. And we that had just arrived in an enormous plane, looking down into the clouds, were left with barf bags filled with the ash from looming infernos. Jung said man doesn't look low enough for God. We climbed down to the basement where the windows were painted between real shadows. When we visited a park to get back to breathing, branches of the winter-dead maple trees on both sides of the narrow ice path entangled in wild foreplay filled our bodies with lust. Under the bridge, the walls were tagged with graffiti we didn't know to read. The sky was no longer in the same place. The moon and stars, drawn much closer, pointed to a grand conspiracy. The river that was in the memory, mangled with pyre-ash, burnt wood, mud lamps and, hyacinth was now clear. We could see the glassy bottom. We could hear the geese flapping the sky. And when I reached for my shadow in the water, the water moved, the shadow shattered as though we were in a dream, walking a prairie of deep freeze, anxious it would all end suddenly and we would be lost. Even when everything is lost is it really everything? Someone said, before we got naked. I opened my head. Then we sat by the river: the water mirrored, the waves pulsed, the wind rarely failed to cut us into pieces. We listened to the red songbirds, four beats to each measure. Like common time. Each beat making up a quarter note until they conjoined, became a whole and washed us in hope. Despair.

The Life of a Shadow

As a shadow, you have no substance, but you have rights. You take no space, but no one can deny you are here. As a shadow, you show up. Your certainty distinguishes you. The moment they open a window you are there, sure as a shadow. Since only you can do that, they make you a plastic horseshoe and hang it around your neck for good omens in the near future. You hold on to it like a trophy—an objet trouvé—your id, ego, superego—your passkey to the lost paradise. Sometimes you land before time into a room floating in ambient lighting and your earnest punctiliousness irritates them. No one wants a shadow in a perfect photograph. You sense it. You leave them alone. Move to the anteroom. You don't want to be over-exposed. But there are other times you miss the train to the final transit, and you are late just when they need you. And in moments of high stakes, if you are nowhere found, that's a whole new room of meta-Freuds. Your absence makes them anxious. *What happened to the shadow? Why don't I see it? Don't I exist anymore?* You tell them your shadow-ness is not about them, but you, the manner you have pointed the arc lights onto your head, they get panic attacks hunting for you inside. Now you act tough, hoity-toity, abstruse. You too have a horse to feed. But you don't overdo it. Because you know if they can't find you long, they'll replace you with another shadow. Or they might stop looking inside, or worse, if the panic kills them and they too become a shadow, your death is certain and utterly painful. No one should die a shadow of a shadow. You know that. So, you rarely raise your hand and almost never stick out your tongue.

Place is a Sentence

1

To prove you are capable of belonging you had to reveal your place. Since they were busy touching different parts of your tongue you could say nothing else. What is place anyway? *The scent of your tilled back garden,* someone said, opened a window. And in the strong headwind when you floated up like a shadow of three pasts, they freaked out. *Place is the pit where you plant your apple seed* someone said, switched on the heat pump. And when you melted into a shadow of four futures, they huddled into a corner and pointed their tasers. *Place is the wire mesh closet where Grandma hides the clotted cream. The sound of bells after dark when the cattle come back to the culvert. Root of licorice. Crushed qahwah. Fried banana flower. Milkweed.* They were speaking all at once. Exhausted, they shut up and stared at you. *Now your turn*, someone said. *I am from a hollow*, you said, *can't you see?* They wouldn't believe it. They took a sample of your spit, asked you to breathe into a device, sent you down a cobbled alley, down three flights to the Department of Interior where someone took off her shirt and pointed at a map beating on the cavity of her chest—a place you didn't even know existed—*that's what you need.* But to have a void filled with an unknown map is pointless. Can I have a feather instead, you said, or leaf, or balloon, anything but a map. The artist said *No, your place on the map is a must-have; you have to serve your sentence.*

2

Later, in the country correctional, rain was pounding windows forever closed, my new fairy godmother was reading from a book. *To be the sucker for a place is to be the fat atlas in the country library no one cares to touch*, almost a rasp, she was having trouble breathing in the loaded air. *You are chained to a turnplate with a perforated head and histories channelling through maps of shame and cuneiform of countless atrocities coded to the rocks of your rivers, is the constant song that wrings your head—a long sentence from which your soul is carved. And because nothing touches the groove of your vinyl record, the sentence swirls like a whip stitch crochet and you are paralyzed.* But my own mother who hung like a shadow behind a ceiling rosette was in the mood for an argument. *To be an alien from a void is to be the finger puppet of rainbows. Without place, the moonstones gathered in your eye bags and the clock hands that play in your sleep have no existence, no alibi; you are a pendulum made from cotton balls and no matter how high up the hills you shoot up, when the wind turns you are thrown back to the school of goats and volcanoes.*

3

By the time I woke up the clothesline had dried, a rainbow chained to the sky. I was in a dim seminary facing the prison pastor dressed in white . . . *In physics* . . . he cleared his throat . . . *a rainbow happens when light having entered water seeks ways to get out to the big ether—like koi in a tin tank—searching ways to get back to big water. And if the body is water and the soul is a wet bulb we must be the flip side of the rainbow for holding on to light. And the alien of a place is a point of inversion. But if the soul is just stone, visible only after tropical storms wash off the water trapped in light, the alien of a place is a prisoner of dark corners, stacked precariously like a cairn that's a burial and a memorial, a marker that's also a museum and the sentence must be served.*

To Rename an Alien

It was always going to happen. I knew way before Belgian supermarkets remade the tomato into the new "clown nose" and researchers in Ithaca remade the carrot into the new "orange rocket" endowed with "Xray vision" and brushed up the zucchini into the new "troll bat" packed with power. I knew they'd trap my mother in manoeuvres of memory—the ministers and members of parliament—clothing streets and bridges, parks and peaks with lost languages and histories. I knew. Because the day I was renamed I lost all memory and was renewed; turned into an ant, trapped in a Mason jar of marmalade made from mamoncillo. And when I was a child although I dreaded that moment when my name got mangled and misinformed in the bramble of periwinkle, like a burn, I ran through a maze of mirrors reflecting broken toys that washed up the ocean marinade. And in the mud, I felt my bones like a broken compass before it misfired. And when I was a boy in the sunset of the sparkly hill and a man newborn in the crackly jack of boxed housing, there was the joy of hide and seek, finding new reflections in the multiplying wombs of all the new mothers. And when I lost my mandibles in an ice cream cup I did nothing about my losses. I agreed without fuss to all the magnificent markers on well-travelled pack sacks. I agreed without protest to all the magnificent creams that reinterpreted my skin. Mornings I jumped out of bed and purveyed new compromises of passage; new meanings of my place projected on mammoth cave walls.

But today I'm done; dead tired, making up my own name. I have run out of shame and the eggs I brought home are crammed with salmonella and the papers I tried to get away from have stuck onto my pants coated in the blood from all my coinciding wars. Today if you call me alien I won't fight you back, call you an imposter or change my name. It was always going to happen. You knew.

On Leaving

Deep inside a familiar town, I have been recruited into an army of comic book ants, doomed to mill around the dumpster until I die of exhaustion—blind, in no man's land, constantly crisscrossing borders and boundaries—my dark nose pointed at the queen holding a shiny compass. Lao Tzu says, *worry how you water a dream*. And when this dream keeps chasing you around the world and recurs in every hotel bed facing a dark TV stood up on a birch-pastel drawer of chests it must be because the arc of your story is the limp shirt on the satin hanger in the hotel closet.

Mother says, *when you forget the past you forget how to water the dream. When will you stop eating lotus? You were not the one to lock your voice in the naked landfill. You were not the one to dunk your soul in batter, fry it in butter, or wrap it in plantain leaves in order to serve the blind queen with a nose for maple syrup. To dunk the tongue in sour cream was not how you wanted to finish supper.* Mother who has never left home, what does she know?

When you remove the dimout sun blinds you. Outside, a Chinese hibiscus explodes a plastic patio. When you believe in leaving, is it the nature of believing that you must go blind? When you know boundaries are fleeting, is it in the nature of knowing that the head blows up like poplar cotton?

Lao Tzu says, *stop thinking and end your problems*. Mother says *the nose that can't see has no dream, no mariposa, nor the fish rotting behind the moon*. Mother says *the bolted head is worse than no head. To escape is to be forgotten. To survive hunger, you stay the ground and haul the coulter. To survive hurricanes, you drop roots deep into the ground. You hear me?* Mother who has done nothing but tended tea roses in the terrace garden, what does she know?

But when I go blind, inside a dream unfolding at a distance, why don't the birds come back? Why doesn't the moss rose, or mariposa, jasmine or marigold, iris or the pergolas of clematis, the rambling rose? Mother who has lost her steps to the terrace reminds me: *here, take some dirt, water the roots. Because when you leave your terrarium you become Sisyphus, and to mill the hill to the end of time is no way of dying*. Lao Tzu says, *without leaving your house, you can know the whole universe*. Mother, who can barely hear says, *do I know Lao Tzu?*

Things to Do in a Tornado

Last night I visited the country where they make pearls from tears. Last night I visited the town where they distract the dying with cappellas about what they remember of the previous life. Last night I was in a forest of charred ironwood falling over each other like Persian mourners.

Once I'm gone and the warren of dim streets fall with their failed hearts, it's no longer ironwood, no longer a forest. That's what they say. But if the failure of the heart is the reason for all the tears in the world, what happens when I dig a trench and enter the dark?

Last night I entered a dark tunnel—not a word, not a spit of blood, didn't move an inch inside my heart—they say it's no longer the same dark nor the same tunnel if you pass over, eyes shut. But if tunnels exist only when I hear walls hiss in my head, darkness must be a delusion.

This morning when I looked at the mirror there was a dim sun and tornado sirens clouded over the constancy of the clock and a storm outside loaded with cries of birds, broken branches, tin roofs like Persian carpets and a shade of grey I had never seen outside a warren of windows.

Yet, I don't believe darkness is different just because a window is blinded by a sheer of glass walls. As if it's a lesser failing if I chain my body to the hands of a clock or stab my heart with the arrow of a compass or puncture my eardrums with the wings of a songbird—run, run, run.

And yet it's not the same sky after storm if all I have done is folded the window, dug trenches with candy canes and carols. That's what I know. The voices speak in different tongues, but they are not nothing or why do dark bags appear under eyes even when everyone's talking?

A Brief History in the Aftermath of the Snatched Tongue

I was accidentally leaning on the balcony of an old fort—yes—one the Brits set up to fight the Indians here, overlooking that eerie lake in New York, when a brick came loose, a mob took over my memory and snatched my tongue. Then, knowing nothing better to do, they set me on fire. Or so I thought, because now I was the accidental Indian being blamed for all the bloodshed. Like any law-abiding citizen, when I reported it to the county police, they said I should visit a psychiatrist. Of course, this happened when I was on the margin of the music sheet, a time stamp among the uninsured. Of course, this is nothing new. Of course, it has happened before, to many others, around the world: their memories stolen along with their eyes and tongues. But this is my brain we are talking about. Not some jagged page in a historical treatise in the Department of Cultural Ethnography at the University of Nowhere. It hurts. And it feels empty like a pile of dead bees at the bottom of a hive—a complete dead out—to have your memory stolen from the hippocampus and other related structures of the prefrontal lobe and replaced with fat English dictionaries hollowed out by mites. The situation became so utterly dire, I had to visit a DIY store immediately after the heist, to have my mouth buttressed with steel braces, inside out. Even after several trips to the gold-arched burger store, there was an empty feeling in the stomach, hunger pangs, insomnia. What was I hungering for? Was it even real or some leftover charge from unused batteries after an odyssey to Mars? Was I manufacturing angst? I wanted to yell out. Realized, I had lost even the basic ability to make familiar speech sounds that my mother could understand. So, I endured, tried to walk around, cut the last paragraph out of my history, made a restart. Inside my tongueless mouth, it was dark. But since darkness comes in waves, as I kept tripping, piles of ash and satin ribbons cushioned my fall. My mother said I should take their advice, see someone. I am feeling the burn, I said. It's a different kind of fire. I can see it—right there—the methane-belching Darvaza of Turkmenistan—a burn hole not to set the soul alight but to frame it in concentric layers of soot. I can smell it in my sleep. Is it a friendly fire, asked the doc, who was Welsh/Scottish/English depending on your ear. Yes. I had become certain the fire was like that landlord who occasionally took the stairs to yell out obscenities from the rooftop before suffering a bout of amnesia. I could swear, it did not touch my body, no butt marks, visible signs of trauma, and yet this horrible, stinging burn. Since the doc had a photo of Freud hanging down his office wall, I wondered if it had something to do with sex or childhood. Freud said dreams are ways to fulfil infantile wishes. So, what was I to make of it . . . I ran towards the mirror. The fire ran with me. I tried to concentrate, feel my skin, arms, head, torso, even the soul at the centre of the solar plexus, a beating heart inside a shadow. Face. Everything. Intact. I ran out the door, towards other patients from all over the world—Philippines, Peru, Panama even São Tomé—crowding over to watch me. First, they made baby sounds, then they made room, then they started fleeing out the window like bees—and as I followed deep inside the dead-out, they were gone, and again I was facing the doc who said he could do nothing about my dead beehive; he wasn't the one who set it on fire. I told him he had no choice. He said I was hallucinating. I leapt out of my seat, jumped on him. He was quick to slide under the table. I hit a wall; tried to turn around; no room. I leapt into the void hoping to land in the eye of the knotted tongue. It was a long, never-ending leap. I don't know if I found something to hold on to—rope or noose—or the fire ended. It was a dream. Dreams are wishes.

How to Fight the Phantom that Hijacked My Voice

First, it was my eyes, then the tongue, now the voice. The shaman looked at the bills I had laid out on the table. It was pity before he cleared his throat. No. You don't fight it like the common cold. Soak your ears in mineral oil. Breathe. No. Not that aspirin. Cut a window here, he touched the thorax. Look out the street. No. Not that broth of clams. No more lemon with honey. No way you can resist voice pirates with pop and potato chips. Open the other window, now he touched the bone between my eyebrows. Feel the phantom coming on full frontal. No, not that lozenge! Don't spray your throat. Nothing you get from the pharmacy can counter the drag of gravity toward complete neurasthenia. Do me a favour—prime your tongue like a catapult, work it constantly. Remember the sounds you made when you were playing the ox dressed up like a monkey. You don't have to make sense, just make sound. But don't' choke. You got to be alive for this. Fly out the window if you can. Imagine wings when you begin to fall. Die once or hold on to the sky. You'll need the salt, spice to staunch the soreness. Sure. Shout down the dirty wind but don't get drowned in your own spit. It's not your head that needs to heal. No Vitamin C. Coneflower Zinc. No more cosmetics for the clogged heart. Whatever you do, keep the branches of your bronchioles open. *Nothing but nature can cure a common cold.* Don't say that. *The clogged voice can't be lost forever.* Don't say that. *I can picture the phantom in the flamed tonsil.* Don't. You got to be sick to think you can melt the ghost in mulled cider and drink it down. Take a warm shower. Use a feather to scrape out the stubborn wax. Keep eyes dry.

Things to Do in Insomnia Motel

Last night I drifted out of the dark by lane and bought a dream book, raided all the countries where I can be at once, and found snow, sleet, hoarfrost, spider plants, coneflowers left out in the cold to play dead until spring.

Last night the streets were rugged with rice husks. The rice was golden brown, enough to feed the town. Hunched up with hunger, I sat folded on the floor, pink nails, blue fingers, curled around tin-coated copper, I stared at the fire, as the wood face of my mother bathed in sweat fell in pieces.

Last night I found moths, woodpeckers, ladybugs, assorted cuts of moon stabbing the great lakes; a vapid moon shaking as swans made love; a raging moon spilling its guts into gutters; a desolate moon angled in oblique depression; drowned in the wild of a lit prairie.

Last night I ate rice with milk and honey. I ate rice with salt and chili. I ate until a princess in Tussah silk stopped by, carrying a tinny echo in the crock. *Come on out. Come on out. Look what I got.* I followed her.

Last night someone said, let's not wage this war of words. Last night someone shouted, words are shallow. Words are shadows in a cave.

Last night fires melted glaciers, birds became dinosaurs, cnidarians became well-versed in levitation. Last night screams from the epidemic filled the arteries of the harmonica. Last night every lane became blind, and I took a break from the blinding night.

And my friends from childhood tumbled out of the woods, trailing closely the princess who gave us all a wooden slipper washed in moony brass and asked us all to look for the matching pair. And we looked. In the barn and on the rafters, in the floor and in the skies cracking down the cladding.

Let's not say another word. Not today. There's enough already said in the libraries of the world. And when the horse cart moved, and the princess left without a word, we, the inheritors of the lonely shoe, still looked. We couldn't just give up looking for luck.

The Curry Shop

At the corner of South Linn and Washington is a consolation, but mostly empty. I entered once but didn't eat, instead, suffering an immediate deflation upon touching the menu, traded stories, conflating places and times. But later that summer, whenever I crossed Madison, Capitol, and Clinton towards College, I'd stop to take a peek before curiosity became a full-blown fixation—a station of hope—to find at least one person inside, the crystal of the tall chandeliers turned on—hoping to avoid the owner's glass eyes, looking out the stainless window searching the length of an empty Iowa Ave. After dark, and again after a tornado, I'd dream—the streets are flooded and I'm stopped under the archway, looking inside, one breath at a time, while the fables are flipped, affairs are floating, and the forfeited Maharajas prised out of their gilded frames are holding on to the rondure of their bosomy consorts. When I shared my feelings everyone said it was the result of an inflammation. Fear of failure, fear of trouble, fear of friendlessness—a kind of poison. Like a snake that cradles poison in its glands, you carry it, oblivious of effect. *You are a snake. And snakes moult when they can't fit their skin. They live in holes bored with forked tongues; their moulted skin is the dust of their dark nights. To be drowned in skin, devoured by skin, to sleep in a moleskin bag is your eternal condition.* But that can't be the whole truth. I protested. Because if I have poison in my glands it's what I forked out the fists of fat dictionaries. And it's not the case that I don't moult, or that my skin has hardened like ants—because—I'm raw—even though I make holes, chew down sugar, build castles and crouch to a queen; deep inside my brain I look like a butterfly. Deep inside the curry shop, on the purple-indigo walls a bejewelled umbrella hangs on a silver peacock head, a cow maneuvers a narrow mud lane and a girl in dark braided hair—back turned to the buffet—faces a large iron door waiting for it to open.

The Colony

The colony must have a Queen. The Queen must make a thousand ermines from a single epiphany. The colony must have workers; workers must fill granaries with bloodstone and sapphire; babysit the brood. The colony must have an army, soldiers must build homes, mind wolves, vampires. Some ants fall prey to vampires, when they find something to chew, they take on a death grip. The colony drags them out of their sanctuaries, damns them, deports them. The colony must have aviators. Drone ants winged at birth must follow their ancient curse, forbidden to mate, immanently love struck, they must fall through the perforated soul into the sperm of virgin princesses, annihilate instantly. Some worker ants have no ears, no tongues. Some ants are blind. All ants have a feel for the fraught ground. The colony must have heirs and wills, devisees, princesses. When the princesses surrender their soul they must also surrender wings. After a single epiphany, they must dig the beaten ground, start a new colony before they can be coronated. And the Queendom spanning miles must forbid memory, must inhabit memory, must fall prey to memory. Worker ants are almost seafoam, drone ants are almost timber, the colony must have no mirrors. All ants seek sugar. All ants must sugar. All ants must haul fifty times their heft. Not all colonies have men. Some men are homeless; some homes are less. The colony's doors are braced with words—*blood, country, poison, scum, go-away*. Queens must know how to count. Queens must make words count. No ant can quit sugar. No Queen can quit the colony. No colony can acquit the Queen.

He Was Alone in a Park

He was alone in a park. We sat shoulder to shoulder, two drunks under a flowering myrtle. Late August, newly arrived, I was looking for work. He wore a pinstripe tux, the kind they rent for weddings. He looked shattered in his gray beret. I made a mistake, purely out of boredom, asked him about love. He looked at me with pity, pulled out a cigar, his hair like a disrupted river, eyes opaque like river stones, he smelled like water fern. It was dark. To love something is to suffer, he said, not like the myrtle in the second bloom, but like the rose, shedding new petals each day to placate the sun. How can you be so sure, I said. He changed his stance on the bench. To love is to suffer, not like a dry inkwell but like the roots of a born-again myrtle searching memories deep inside the dirt. Why should I believe in contraries, I said. Now he stood up and paced the length of the tree's shadow, like the joker in the circus that had already left town. To love something is to suffer, not like a church bell but like a dry inkwell waiting like Caesar to be stabbed before it can become a mirror. Lies. I said, touching the sour burns with my cigarette tongue. He grabbed my collar, almost choking me. To love something is to suffer, not like excavated statuary mirroring forgotten rivers but like the tongue of a bell flagellating the naked skin until blood. He offered me a piece of gum. It wasn't a real gum made of zebras, just twisted words. When I sucked on it, my tongue lit up like a volcano. Why did you do that? Unfazed, he said, to ask for love is to ask for lighted coal, ash and dark cloud, holm oak and bracken, vent of tea tree, lava. With those words he rose from the bench and walked, left to right, as in a stage, frequently bowing to inaudible applause. Wait, I said. What does it even mean? He kept walking until the night ate him.

Once I Boarded a Spice Train

Once I boarded a spice train. It wasn't a dream. Because the marble mausoleums were real and the museums crammed with objects of art—in shapes of roots and postures of love—were still being separated from the dirt excavated out of ancient pits. In forests of sugarcane and sorghum women clad in mirrors and bells were dancing to a haunting ballad lost in childhood. And out in the fields, the scarecrows with heads of straw and coal black eyes were blowing wet kisses. Those coal-black hungry bulbous eyes kept me awake as they were kept awake certainly by centuries of snoring in the black sun. And in the face of their sudden beauty, when I stopped the train and fell on my knees and begged to be saved, the dancing women among the scarecrows said nothing. Not a word when I took one of them in embrace or tied myself in chains around another—its straw body crackling as if it was tickled to laughter even as I drowned myself in tears laced with mood music. And then I took a deep breath and looked down my plastic horror. It wasn't a dream. Because the flaming rivers clogged with dead shadows were real, and the volcanoes festering with unclaimed blood flowed everywhere, and the countless coins trapped in the watercress were algae-green and in the pyramids of pith, I could hear a long winding requiem of all my voyages from near and distant past. And when the train reached its destination, I found ice balls dipped in crushed rainbow.

Upon Meeting Kafka in a Country Café

Ghosts from ancient history that travelled the silk route and spice route, tin route and amber had perverted my dreams with their steamy incense. Night after night I dreamt of the sugar castle and slept in the womb of the mayor's wife. When the sun warmed up the satin sheets and I found the glossy towers climbing up the clouds and the stockinged windows opening to the jackdaws, I knew I had come of age. When I found the invisible crack and penetrated the wall, they found me, and I felt on my neck the sharpness of their blade. In my death, I blamed instinct, my sugar cult. And when I was born again—just as resilient as ancient travellers of infinity—and went about in stolen boots following footrails in the ice, the shadow of the castle pressed into my heart like a knife. To hear time, you must step into the river twice. In my failure to breach the castle, I blamed my eyes. Was it me dreaming the castle walls or the walls dreaming of me? I forgot. The guards said it'd be better I stopped blaming them for the rot in my memory. And when I pointed at the feathers in my tongue they pointed at my clotted eyes. Later that afternoon, when I met Kafka in the country café, it was gloomy. But when I showed him mappings of my past voyages—no dates or markers, just an illusion of wisdom—he wrapped his arms around me, as if together we had fulfilled a lengthy dream, as if the shiny castle walls playing up sugar ants as showy trifles was part of his original plan.

Models of Migration

Sugar ants from sunset bring bad luck reflected in old mirrors; troubles echoed in hoarse bells inside whitewashed temple domes; debts that inhabit the marrow of history; hunger that lives inside guts like feral dogs howling forever.

Sugar ants from sunup bode better: for repayment of debts; from down south they bring gold, silver; from up north they bring winds that drive the river down to the milk of estuaries. That's what they say. What do I know? I was taken by the winds and trapped in ant colonies since 1763.

Some sugar ants stay still, some are peripatetic, moving forever in the direction of the wind. Some carry eggs in their crocks, some quietly quit the galley, when they see a lip in the ship kissing a turgid moon. Some have noses like lighthouses; some know tides; music of waves; some know when it's time to adjust the clock, anchor, compass; what the seashells say to the clam, what the owl says to the woodchuck, things of that kind.

Some have learned to levitate for hours, spanning epochs and continents; some are fake prophets with tinny voices hovering rivers decorated with chalk flowers of the dead. Some lay out lily-livered lyrics; some are like the loveless toads that the moon opened up. Some never tire of doing nothing, some are like the chak chak of the tin boat searching roots of lotus. That's what I know. And I know, all ants crave sugar. All of them sugar.

On the Commute to Work

One day I forgot my glasses and everyone in the mourning green train car looked like they had escaped their bodies—heads constantly moving like a spring toy—here, there, yesterday, tomorrow—as if they were all suffering the same existential OCD—the constantly metamorphosing idea of who, where, why, when, coded to the beat of the heart same as the burr of the train.

One day I forgot my eyes and everyone in the car smelled like vetiver, mimosa, leather and the coffee bean aisle at the grocery; jointed at the navel, steaming hot dog buns in both hands I heard birdsong in the growls of the empty stomach where I feared I had trapped a scorpion.

One day I forgot to screw my head tightly and when the train skidded on ice and my head came off I was dead for a moment before I wiggled back into a head that had rolled onto my feet; hot like inferno, this new head couldn't do even basic things—recognize the clothes I was in—before everyone jumped into a communal hug—touching and smelling all over.

Time ran out. The station arrived. We were pushing out the door still conjoined like a twenty-foot tongue of a Latin ant eater when someone tapped my shoulder . . . *you are wearing my head . . . here's yours* . . . Back in my eyes, clothes, familiar vestibular sense . . . so embarrassing . . . how could stolen heads be ablaze in the same inferno? We split like atoms and hurried to the Convention Hall.

Soul and Hunger

What's the soul? I asked. The Master moved blueberry beads between thumb and forefinger. *It's a beast. Lives here*, he said, pointing at his potbelly. I was hungry, but the insult made a knot in my throat. And before I could find a voice, the Master had moved on, musing over the menu card fitted with tinny mirrors. *You see it after the fast. But no one should be fasting if they have nothing to dig, discover or discard.*

But Nietzsche said, the soul is not the Goddess excavated from ancient mounds, it's the chant of weary shoes on shiny cobblestones. To hear the chants, one must be at work, awake. I didn't have to say it; the Master could read my thoughts. And if my soul is not the sun on my face and my face is not the shadow floating on the teacup and my body is not even the naked pith holding the curved water, what should I do? Can I know anything at all?

The soul is an ice cream cone, the Master shut his eyes, slurped on his saliva. We could smell food already. *And why is that?* I wasn't going to let him get away with sugar-coated words. But the Master had moved on, running an ivory comb over his pate. *And no one should be licking up on an ice cream cone in public unless you want to murder someone . . . Because the sea salt in the caramel enters your vents, titillates your tongue, puts you to sleep the moment you start driving.*

Denied food for days after digging for dead tubers, the congregation was restless. *But there isn't always cream at the bottom of the cone*, I punched the air as someone pushed me out of his way. And to reach the bottom, mustn't the sugar be broken down to the chocolate plug? And if the cone has no bottom and the excavated cup doesn't wiggle with worms, what use is in reaching the end?

Let's eat, the Master said.

The Truth About the Root Cause

I knew everyone was lying. And the lies came in all colours. I wasn't homeless, just hungry. Hunger is no stain except it tastes like poisoned lead. I arrived at the lead because I had fallen off the bed and as I was crawling, the floor was painted cardinal. Beyond the threshold, beyond the walls, beyond the rafters, I had come for a curved horizon. The sky was a contradiction—a pale blue that went dull grey before the dark sun dried out. At night they asked me to show my hands: *what have you got*? I had nothing to hide; showed them my tongue transcribed with the history of hundreds of invasions. *And how did you survive?* They said they were going to take me to the lab; have my lineages looked at. I had something else, I said. When I took off my shirt someone reached into the hollowed centre—grooved like a long play vinyl—hijacked my record and phoned in for a ransom. But there was no one on the other side to answer the call. I did come in debt; not disaster; I did come to do a bid, not for the joy; just a sugar rush. I had to survive. They couldn't understand my passage even after I played an old mantra that moderated my past possibilities and potential; steeped my daily sentences. Weighed down by a useless tongue I failed all the tests of grammar. But my skin hung out like a paint run. And all the colour words were rooted in mud. I didn't come to root or gather new rings in my grooved, l-p chest, so it didn't matter where they pointed the ladder. I climbed down to the sugar pit, filled a music sheet and sang the choir. Even though I came hollow, I didn't come empty, I said. Look how my past has followed me. They said it was all my fault; a hostage of sugar walls, lead had stained my blood.

Ode to Lost Mothers

Easily angered. *Don't get too close to incense and holy water*, she says, before bathing the Gods in lime juice and vinegar, feeding them fruit and sugar. She's glad they'd never come alive, nor ask questions. *I have no one to answer.* She watches them grow fat, their pot bellies expanding in the sun filtering through a clothesline curved under the weight of fresh washings clinging the shapes of people supposed to have been still here, long gone. She dresses them in silk and pith, nickel ornaments; conjures from a dream book forgotten rivers that might have flowed for over eight millennia into an estuary of buttermilk, rubbing sandalwood on a round soapstone before she smears the paste on their faces—stone-cold—clay hands and feet—and with the rest of the long afternoon she rolls incense sticks, lead gray, impaled into a slice of rotten apple. *Don't let them too close*, she says of the matchbook before struggling to light the fire and again repeats, bending over the candle to put the fire out. With the spilled wax she plugs holes in the burned carpet and sits watching the smoke consume the tabernacle, murmuring an ancient script marked with sounds she no longer understands. When the smoke clears, tears from the eyes of the brass peacocks teleport into her, she raises her head and bites into the remaining apple rescued from rot.

To Leave the Lion Face Stranded

To leave the lion face stranded in the dark tunnel, push the last pieces of purslane into peat oil, twist steel toes into memory, leave a mark on the habits, shred useless anxieties about futures and commodities, burn with flame-throwers, feed ashes to the big spruces and excuses, bury the disasters in the dead slow river, chain the tongue, take the skin, squeeze the failure out of sun, nail the shadow soul in the slough like sumac bitter sweet horsetail and thistle, smoke it like Sour Diesel, I shall build the church of the Bubba Kush on the mopboard of mallow. Who said the Golden Goat can't be broken? Or burnt? Who said the Northern Lights have no limits? Or cannot die? You forgot the alien is me and sugar ants are older than dinosaurs. Hard like hemlock, handy like fruit pebbles, pineapple express, in all seasons: euphoria, nausea, pain, distress.

I'm here to stay.

The Seven Circuits

The groom arrives on a hired horse trailing a drum roll of polished brass, the bride's mother blesses him ten thousand things, families exchange strings of cultured pearl, embrace. O Ganesha, clear the obstacles! The priest's Sanskrit races high winds before the bride appears on a palanquin—face covered in betel and sandalwood—the groom and bride look at each other, in awe, as if they were in a temple of minor gods—exchange garlands of pith and garden flowers. A fire is lit. The bride's father gives away the gardener's hennaed rose. And then they walk the seven circuits with vows to nourish and to share; to be and to grow; care as friends; preserve what's theirs.

By evening the bride is again on a pedestal, draped in brocade and filigree, cut heads of night lily, and the groom on a gilded highchair is caked in cascarilla. It's that hour, they know, shall never repeat. Not even if they were to breathe back the vows and walk the seven circuits in reverse. And that's the truth. Since truth is in the pit of fire and truth is also in the dazzle of silk and stone, beauty that can visit only once in a lifetime, must be a different kind of truth.

As night claws back the high windows, and candles burn pinholes on high mirrors, in the traffic of naked wing pits crawling the aisles of curry and kebab, in the cherry tongues slurred by grape and malt, in the smoke from all the lip-stained cigarettes, in the frozen smiles on painted masks there's a studied beauty hung like curtains of velvet burgundy down faux ceilings of wood and gypsum, hope strikes in flashes of thunder on a printed shamiana.

After all the storms in every teacup, raindrops shall shine like the diamond tiara on the bride's head! O Ganesha, make it happen! Hope is prayer. And now you are married, the priest declares. And that's the truth. And the truth about the bride's tiara is the truth of the mica in the naked midriffs and the perfume of sarsaparilla and the icing on the tiered cake and Portello—a portent of things to follow—a promise of an expanding granadilla out in the dark milk—solemn like a shiny shoe that the bride's sister must steal so the groom can't go to bed and whisper into the stalks of the potentilla. Not quite yet.

Because words have choked the heart, and eulogies must be read aloud. And then everyone's twirling like Sufis outside memory and the rain-wet window is one crystal candelabra. In the hour of wild drums, the prosody of the ever-lost home is clear. Awake to the jocks' fingers on the clarinet's intractable nipples, rapt in beat, all bodies move in step like a singular showboat in a slow river moon to squeeze through the yellow lotus chalked on the red mandala.

Outside, sparklers pop and a meteor from a faraway galaxy swoons down in flames to merge with the dirt of the azaleas. In the hour of being weightless and wet—sweaty with syrup and Bollywood—the hour of amethysts and heliotropes—you feel immortal like a ghost squeezing into gaps between memory and dream, fudge and taffeta. In the hour of becoming—suspended like a cellophane star—you are timeless and eternal. And as all the brothers sleeve up to push the getaway fjord, the bride and her mother can't hold back tears.

The Crows from Childhood

You take a right on Bloomington, neighbourhood of white clapboard homes and plastic wheelbarrows, you hear nuthatch, red cardinal, tufted titmouse on the phone; across the street, a black family of four with a nylon rope are in animated conversation—about to hang something, or anchor, tie, secure or shackle—while a noisy lawn mower makes things even in the sun.

Up north, the street opens to windows of rustic wood and careful craftsmanship, doors of depth and character, like well-plotted novels, bigger decks and curated lawns, but I am not here to own anything. On the street, ants and discarded condoms, and right by the park, a sign that says Hickory Hill, and a man in a messy bib on a ladder with a pail of paint.

Inside, wildflowers, broken maple and blooming yarrow, empty benches, hint of a water that I am told is Ralston Creek.

Further up, along the North Star, an obstacle course of sawed logs, smell of dog pee, chickadees, house wren and a union of cicada broods not seen since 1803. Someone foraging mushrooms. Disrupted signal. Fear felt first in the bones before breaking into a wave of sweat not seen in decades.

I read somewhere the biggest threat to this Prairie in progress is urban deer and the feet of visitors from far away, walking off trail, curiously stabbing with their feet the visible underbelly of the sloping gullies becoming since 1927. To the west, a cemetery full of dead Iowans.

Deeper inside, northern parula, robin, warbler, mosquito, and dog walkers. And as the trails move in and out of the wild, the fear of losing way transforms into a believable trust, almost faith-like, in the world turning in short arcs of incitement, continuity, climax and return to the full circle.

At the edge of the park a patch overlooking a raised perch that you want to cross instantly, if only to reap the diamonds off the grass, an unusual green; on a boulder etched cursive: *remembering is an act of love*. Deeper inside, unknown. Hundreds of foot-stabbed paths woven round and round the belly of a recovering wood. Butterflies. The sound of leaves flapping. A beaver dam but no beavers.

Later on, several miles away from the red tornado-safe-room, house finch, house wren, sparrow and a boy called Jack, about six or seven, who stops you out of impulse or trust or faith or hope, I don't know, to point at his mama plucking false sunflower at a crossing two blocks from the farmer's market where they sell a small bottle of smoked *Awesome* for fifteen dollars.

And in between all this walking to and from the wildflowers back to the bazaar of Latin jewelry, kitchen-table-art, back garden zucchini and green apple, back to the rented house where windows never shut and ants nest everywhere, there is another kind of walking that is neither to nor from anywhere or anytime, nor across, along or around—beyond prepositions of movement—a walk to a strange kind of identity that has nothing to do with skin, colour, or morpheme.

A walk towards prepositions of stillness—if there are those ever invented in the grammar of daily transactions—towards repose, not singleness but totality, not death—and not because the Hickory Hill cemetery is all but full—but to an inner coherence—from the echo chamber of history to the leaf song of finch and love songs of sparrow and nuthatch.

Sparrows, I am told, can swim underwater but cannot walk until they achieve certain wisdom, and the nuthatch walk headfirst on the side of trees so they can reach places other birds miss, and when you think about that you are bound to wonder if all this walking through plains and prairies is about moving inside headfirst to find things otherwise missed, or to swim in and out of triumph or resignation, privilege or abjuration, arrival or exile?

And when you think of that, you remember the gnawing of beavers on rotting wood, piles of sticks and the ingenious dams of debris, but no beaver; and you realize how absence takes up space, how emptiness hangs like a frame around the world shot from outer space by the Hubble telescope, and then you hear the crows of Hickory Hill in your dream, only the crows, for those are the only birds you can recall without reference, ever present, like war reporters, embedded into every turn since childhood.

At the Supermarket

Apples are American, but Bananas are Guatemalan. The Tibetan Black Diamond apple, the rarest of rare, is actually purple, stocks are red and green on monitors overhung; cakes are chambered in the arcade of parfait; the yard is inflamed with mums, here the gloss on the rotisserie is sweet maple. Watermelons are mostly Spanish; the greens are juiced in mist. Grapes are Chilean and everyone's suddenly angry about their flappy wrists: teachers, writers, actors, sailors and now dockhands. All gone down the aisle marked down with yellow icebergs and crinkly tomatoes overlooking a carton marked *landfill* crammed with expired nutrition and infant formula. Lemons are Peruvian and olives are pitted in the aisle next to Lebanon. Oranges are Egyptian. Strawberries are from Saskatchewan, and nectarines from China were invented 2000 years ago from a tarty peach. The Salvation Army guy dressed in Death Star holds a candy cane and a lightsaber. Talking heads talk on glass walls, nonstop. Sims are pre-paid; the laundry rack creaks under ironed sleeves. Pineapples are Honduran. Tea is Indian. I place the tea beside my son on the shopping cart after he accidentally crashes into Toys and rips a Tarot card called Reward. When the clerk insists on reparation I say, I'm new here. I was born in a leaky cap outside a fish market and now, I am worse, since I have been eating mushrooms for breakfast, monsters for supper. She cracks up on trust. Avocados are Michoacán, vinegar is Russian. At the door, a man with ratty hair, and a rubbish bag argues with Security before someone says something about his trappings and belongings; now everyone cracks up. Canned custard is from the United Kingdom. Chocolates are from Belgium. We who are from nowhere, ogle the screen, as an attendant scans the lotto draws, very carefully.

On a Leaf, the Ants

On a leaf, the ants are drinking up rain. They're drinking up. They're drinking up. Back in their colony, the queen has split a vein. Devastated by the limits of their canticles they're drinking up.

On a leaf, the ants are drinking up the altar wine. They're drinking up. They're drinking up. Their queen is floating in a dixie cup. Anxious about their heft, worth of their prayers, terrified of the dirge echoing in their heads, they are drinking up.

On a leaf, the ants are drinking up grace. Their heads made of hand-wound clocks have lost all hands. They are drinking up. They are drinking up. Their tongues have lost the stomach for salt.

Night is about; an angry frost has kissed the white lilies. The ants are drinking up. They're drinking up. Today the ants won't head back home. They have no more strength to rewind the clocks.

On a leaf, the ants are drinking up rain, terrified by the tongues of night, they are afraid to open their mouths—one false breath and they shall all drown in the pool of their own shadows.

On a leaf, the ants are drinking from the screeds. A strip of glim coiled in their eyes—today the ant is on the moon. When the skies break, they watch the bees, conjure a new queen—utterly beatific.

On a leaf, the ants have drained the rain. Tonight, they'll dig new ground, cast after the dead. How can anyone be ant and not hope for beauty? How can anyone be ant and not drown in a leaky head?

On Their Five-Step Meditation

After they broke my door and took me along with other quarter-folded aliens, underground, I broke into a glass tank and found what I had heard was true. Some ants have mastered the art of pointing a golden light between their eyebrows, moving deliberately, as if they know the way of matter, the mind of worms, the tongue of plants, making God look almost palpable with a minimal flutter of the tailfin. Might it be harder to be trapped in a lightbox than a dark warren? Theirs seemed like a weird idea of freedom: shut your eyes to ogres from the past; dunk in the water and wait; level with the sun; count till ten; feel grace flowing through orifices. In that fish tank, when you glide past ants made up like lighted fish—the mollies, guppies, tiger barbs, and Oscars—you realize the limits of your own existence, instincts—and the more you get it, the more you want to stop the cycle of prey, play, procreate; be like them. Not because you woke up from sleep. Because it's hard foraging sugar for the queen 24/7. But after some time when the fish skin feels cozy, and they start noticing; nudging you for answers; instantly you are outed like an imposter because the thing you have pointed between your eyebrows is no golden light—it's the shadow you are trying to escape. Because you are no fish. Because your past is not a wish. You know that.

Seabass

An opal seabass torn open by osprey attracts flies It's not summer yet Waves fall dead at a distance The surf holding crushed bones of clams and oysters is cold as a death wish I am with a little girl hopping over dredges filled with rot water still angry about three messengers in a story that ends without warning She cartwheels on sand until a boy points his metal finder at the flaming heart of the dead seabass No she won't look at spilled guts either The boy looking for history settles for broken shells imperfectly rounded stones blanched limbs of fallen trees that look like spat-out dinosaur bones from prehistory We overcome sorrow shock disgust Stop and look Perfectly symmetrical ribs wrapped in silver teeth tight with terror clenched jaws drawn up like cables of steel bladder like gold ingot It's clear the seabass fought hard and lost No one says a word We dig a grave in silence Waves palaver Our hands wilted from digging have turned rock-algae and like always our grave has turned up shallow Waves keep coming after waves like lightning bolts from heaven Nothing else happens No sand can't hold on to heaven

The Stopped River

By the time we returned, the river had stopped. It wasn't a failure of God alone or the ruined robes of preachers. Not the bitter acids in the partisan trench or the cinder in the sibyl's eyes. Not the shattered spine after the steep climb or the weight of water after centuries of gravity. It was about the manner in which the sun had set. Is there going to be nothing after this? The child was anxious.

When no one listened, he posed his question again and again, his tongue wagging like an ancient church bell. When no one spoke, he cried like someone who had just heard death rattle his mother's ruined bones. No one knew how to console him.

Then his mother asked for ink, a blank sheet, plain water. Painted a river that shone like a lamp on a rainy afternoon and licked up the pale sky. And in the river, she planted blithe waves. And down the stream, toward the edge of the sheet, she planted a little whirlpool that moved like a furry one-eyed animal. And between the waves, she planted a dark shadow of our sunk history.

At a Street Play About the Soul

Someone said, scientists have created a camera to film soul particles as they leave a cold body. It happened yesterday. And as they were being presented the Nobel prize, my mother looked up from her crewel work. *But the soul is a slice of sapodilla*, she said, *sweet when you smell it, stones when you don't.* Earlier, in a moment of distress, someone dressed up like the Buddha held up a white flower and twirled about the stage. It was clear he had something important to say but had forgotten his lines. And when the crew tried to bring him back with improvs like . . . *you live like a wave; you hear the sea heave . . .* some soul-crushingly serious cynics watching theatre from the sidelines were harder to convince. They tried to confuse the actor with lines of their own: *there is nothing left in the snot rag after you are dead. You are a bag of bones, mould on the sky-milk. Forever fucked. Alone in your scaffolding of protein and carbon, all your tears and all your blood add up to nothing*. Now another serious-looking actor holding the soul-cam high up on a box ladder, trapped in the ringtone of constant gunshots offered a different take. *Not one more word about drawknives and wooden spoons. What's inside worn clothes and worn buttons is not soul butter but pure memory.* No one could understand him. But since the soul-cam had the soul captured they put the thing on a loop like a lightning flash consisting of three strokes, lasting about 0.1 seconds. It was hard not to pay heed or to deny the failed actor a second chance to twirl about with a white flower. *And oh boy! How did we even get here*, my mother said. As one crazy scene followed another, I realized what they had done to the soul was clearly too simple, almost childish, it made me nervous. *OMG! OMG! the soul?* I was suddenly laughing like a frisbee because I knew a legit soul-shot had only to look a certain way—a blinding mass of light, or a pleasure doll with thunder-spitting breasts that you could squeeze or a lover you knew you would come back to at the twirl of the pirouette. Of course, we were nowhere near the end of the play—myriad characters were still acting out compulsive obsessions about the soul's multi-voiced polyphony—neither were we at the point of origin. We were somewhere in a muddle—unsure if the soul-cam was for real, if the soul sound was a true fake, if Buddha really did what he was supposed to do—act without words—unsure if we have been witnessing a true farce—a lie that we live outside of us or after us—a lie that we trough and crest like light in a chinquapin when everyone's looking and when no one is. And frankly, all these lies, the weight and stink of it all, was a distraction, a drain on the mind so intense I fell asleep before the play got over but my mother who has forgotten the past had no trouble staying awake.

In the Country Sanatorium

In the country sanatorium, where a lost generation tries to piece from feathers the songs of birds that hit the high windows, my mother writes in cuneiform, the first page of her memoir about basalt and rhinestone, gold carpets and red rubies hidden in tin boxes, whims and wax dolls festering in dark family vaults. Her Godless days are weighed down by love stories from broken Tagore songs playing ad nauseum between ads, nausea, and long pauses; she can connect in fits with recordings of nightingales and other tropical birds. *They are trying to silence me with sugar;* she says. When I show her photos of silver chalices, floormats of sabra, embroidered silks, quilted taffeta she had to leave behind, she nods at the little red knife with a hundred points someone brought her from Switzerland. She barely remembers her name. And when I show photographs of her kissing wildflowers, sitting on a wet park bench under a dulcet moon bridge, inside a diner eating grits and cornball, in treacherous rain and on wounded rocks, she responds with morphemes of meaningless words. Only silence sings louder. To reach past her cactus veil is to baptize the dark. But occasionally she stands by the window transfixed by stray dogs howling all afternoon. And when the TV fills up with oceans and mountains, skies and beaches, quickly she's tired . . . *enough*. To rake up the past is to pull out the tongue. To speak about afterlife is to open a new wound. Priests of ash and sandalwood who insist there's nothing wrong with her, locksmiths who claim they can make new keys for her armoire, clock makers who claim they can change her calendars, doctors who claim they can write up a new circadian are *frauds* . . . Time to finish what you started, I remind her. She runs her hand on the blank of the page, the blank of her face, before she stands by the window, watching the street, where stray dogs burn a hole in the night with their howling.

The Newspaper Is a Folded Gun

At the city terminal, when a man boards a train in war fatigues no one cares to give him a second thought, even though he deserves it, even though it's plain obvious there's a war out—he has been fighting someone—before he pulls it out of his backpack—the newspaper is a folded gun.

He struts along the packed corridor pointing it like a—51Fifty—3rdGenTactical—threatening with his looks anyone who dares ignore him. Up and down the train, pacing urgently, as if he's worried he's nobody without menace as if he's certain he'd be soon forgotten before I say *will you sit down*?

Because I'm looking at the electric corn, face pressed hard against the glass of the train window, his shadow like a pendulum keeps reminding me of the past. Whereas I want to forget, searching the pastoral for women dressed in leather and braided blond, mirrors and dancing bells, painted in the primaries of Rothko.

Jung said dreams are whispers from the soul. I am OK. I seem to be holding on—along with bags and belongings—also to my soul. At least the soul is not a lie. Of all the lies I have to navigate lately, to be talked out of the soul would be a certain calamity. I know. I can swallow darkness, skin, but to inhabit a dead soul is a lot.

I'm rolling the happy hammock; roiling with lust; staunchly oblivious as our little universe inside the train moves through the hair comb of sorghum and sugar cane. Surely such beauty is for a reason. Surely there's meaning in being here. Purpose in the present. Until he wakes me up with a whack—that man with the newspaper folded like a gun.

It's obvious he has shot someone. *What's your name?* He asks, distracted for a moment by my wiry shadow framing the four-foot-long beard from ancient history. Surely I am not afraid. Surely my voice is clear. Surely I'm not muffled with slow vowels. Surely I haven't forgotten, just unwilling to reveal the place I'm from.

Strangely, the automatic fires—having refused to name my history I am in a heap—like the Dead Souls of Gogol, not really dead, only, pretending. Because it's obvious the gun is unreal like the news. But when my blood spills out and begins to roll with the rake, nothing is no longer obvious.

Everything is true and nothing is. At least everyone else is alive. But what of them if *I* am dead. Long after the man with the newspaper folded like a gun is gone, my blood flows, I can see it, like a transcendentalist, detached from my body, it's surreal how the plot thickens—hard as rock—I can't stem the hardening of the rot.

Studies of a Wound Under Flashlight

At a gathering of aliens dressed as exotic birds, someone said *a wound is a broken star that found its orbit*. The neighbour's boy—12? 13?—hired as the communal babysitter for the duration of the meeting—had been planning to start a colony in Proxima B—he jumped the man dressed like a toucan. *Broken stars are the brightest*, the boy said. The Toucan who opened the poem stood in visible pain. He had popped an olive into his mouth and was struggling to get the stone out of his throat. *Well, don't you see the halo?* The boy strutted about a Peacock on the piano as the man stopped playing to get another fill of vodka to wash down the bitters. *Wound is the essential matter of memory* added a Puffbird with a Pinocchio nose, gathering with bare hands nutshells thrown to the floor. *Not really the matter* corrected the Cockatoo who had so far been quiet, searching misplaced car keys *but the glue and the gravity mistaken for the marrow of memory*. She had a trident tattooed on her forehead. *What about the broken star?* The boy was adamant. *Go down to the basement, will you?* He wouldn't be evicted without an answer. *What about the broken star?* He went about like a broken record. Everyone stared at the Toucan who had opened the vein. No one knew what to do with the boy. No one could think of the next line. *I was asked to bring just one lie to the party* the Toucan complained. *What do you think?* The gathering turned towards the boy. *Well, won't you do something to restart the star's dead heart? . . . Like what?* No one knew what the boy was after. *Like this*, he flashed his phone at the wall. *You restart a broken star with light*. Everyone shut up for a while. Then they fished out their phones, turned the flashlight on and waited for the Toucan as he peeled his shirt back to the wound, ready to become a star about to explode.

At a Picnic on the Day of National Reconciliation

After a week of larks, the park overlooking a pond where bird watchers from all over gather to take pictures of their loved ones with black duck and blue-winged teal is now taken over by new Canadians from Syria, India, Palestine and Pakistan. Pushed into the back room of the country museum where they hoard erased portraits and paused collectibles, almost forgotten unless it's time to relieve the bladder, a wind-swept Jack Pine gathers dust. Spring has touched a green on the lavender field. A cloud stains the crystal country horizon where a picnic is laid out on a stainless sheet—the colour of dandelion. Slowly, a piece of cloud that started like a ponytailed horseman takes the shape of a slow electric train running from pale red suburbia into deeper suburbia, a carriage of two or three rakes before the wind stretches it from both ends to the point of tear, a many hundred miles, a shade of coal, as if it were carrying dark blood ripped out of gnomes, sylphs and salamander. The sun is about to set. The sooty goods train threatens to run over curated private gardens of lilac and amaryllis surrounding a clump of cottage yards facing each other with pools of still water, acrylic mirrors and Chinese songbirds planted asymmetrically between fifty-year-old pines, maples and ponderosa. Visitors dressed up in elsewhere fuss over a tin sun, whirlies, wind chimes made from broken stones and a triangular parrot in a glass box. In the far corner, a plastic flowering rose stands in atonement beside a stone Buddha. Now the cloud is a sloth of bears charging at a warren of limp plastic huts furrowed by the stench of human waste. It's getting dark. Stories of occupations here and elsewhere have started to meander. Luckily, meat is on the grill, habanero peppers are battered in beer, corn is shucked and silked, and lights are fitted to a pointy parasol to scare away the bears.

Lookalike Tyrant

In the 5th Street Grocery owned and operated by ants, the tyrant on the reading glass aisle looked like me, as with novels with similar story arcs, different settings. Then I found the face splayed on TV, hair products, on cellphones in the corner aisle. What's going on? Are they targeting me? Same hooded eyes, creases, warts: undoubtedly mine. *You can't fool them much longer.* I realized a clerk was following me as I found my way to the counter. *It's an accident,* I said: *a twin exchanged at birth, a body clone.* I realized I had started to run. *Stop lying,* she stopped me. *Are you not the one who got with them and sealed your doorways with cayenne and curry powder, sprayed cumin in our colonies and camps? Isn't that you who colluded with them and stacked your closet mahogany with medals from medical experiments on our spinal cord? Look at the tattoo. Were you not the one who leaned over the gurney begging the nurse to put in a pink heart after they found a splintered mirror with the painted moon in the hollow of your chest? Look at the T-shirt. Wasn't that you who wanted to make new after we were tossed over the wall? Were you not the one who forced us to jump into the freezing lake so you could qualify to be added to the honour roll for the ousting of us: hidden inside the corner of eye puffs, tunnelled inside the sugar fat, stuck in the storm drains under the brain's ambient railroads. Don't forget. The tyrant is you even in that ritzy hairdo. Wasn't it you who said history is meant to be had with popcorn like a horror western? Were you not the one canvassing outside City Hall with the drug lords giving away poisoned syringes? Were you not the one on the science channel threatening a cycle of evolution from our source blood? What's that music? Look at your tote bag, let's see what books you are carrying, open it.*

Card Players in a Train

When it comes to pests only a few can match Colorado's striped beetles, someone says, drawing up an ace from a deck of oriental patterns. They devour everything: potatoes, tomatoes, eggplants, and peppers. They adult in twenty-one directions. Up to three generations cycle up and down the same levers in one season. They are up on every History channel dressed like despots. Thank goodness there are spiders, says another, drawing a Jack. And mites. Spider mites eat beetles. When it comes to appetite none can match the spider mite. And when the train rolls into the capital, past masked demonstrators marching with flags downside-up, someone says the marchers are for those who belong to Animal Farm. We who have no place draw up new flashcards after cleaning the gossamer off the train window. The spiders fight back. Ants don't fight. We have no fight left; it's a fact. We adjust our line of sight, headphones. Of course, it's a shame but no fault. No one taught the sugar ant how to duel the striped beetle, the spider mite. *Stay on your track. History is a circle. This too shall pass.* This radio plays only back songs. And when the train passes a square where sugar ants are out on the streets fighting spiders with doorknobs and broken armchairs someone says *What do they know*? And when we see ants in beetle-infested hop farms shooting at the hot sky . . . *What do they know?* And when we hear back from Animal Farm about those who died fighting pigs with sheets and saxophone . . . *What do they know?* What do we know: want and fear. What if the beetles eat up our potatoes? *When there's beetles, pray for spiders, when there's spiders pray for pirates. When there's pirates pray for pigs.* When the train ramps up and the window recedes, we stop playing, draw the blinds down, dim the lights, open that weedy Mason jar.

Winter Bird

In deep December, you walk out to the crunch of snow, ice floe in the frozen river, a trail pocked with moon craters and frozen torch lily, navigating an unfamiliar language of inflected intervals. When you turn, you have lost your way. When you return, the room you left behind is not the same, the mirror that reflected your face only a while back is not the same mirror, even the frozen bird nest that branches out the heart of the frozen window looks like a giant tarantula spinning its web, not yet ready for sacrifice, but to take you in its resolve to never freeze, devour you. All of a sudden you are in the gut of an alien winter bird—finch-siskin-junco—broken down by acids, organs of usefulness and pragmatism—having lost your way to the wild, having lost your way back, you know you can no longer be the centre of your own universe, mirroring your light. Now you are a talon in the bird-claw, a hair in the bird-head, not useless but raw, exposed, stripped of the last piece of identity, paralyzed. When you wake up it's late. How did that happen? How could you let it? You who had started out dreaming of daisies since childhood, to end up being the underfur of an unknown snowbird roosting in a frozen bird nest on a leafless maple sounds like failure. You turn and turn like a windsock. There is no one else inhabiting your voice; no one else walking. Your eyes echo the hollow wind but what was the choice? Those who say the moon is mirror, the river is clock, the night is compass, don't know a thing about the moon, or mirror, clock or compass.

Things They Do To You At The Airport

Maybe I'd arrived late. They were pointing at their clocks, then they took me to the corner room and asked me to strip. *Why?* We do this to everyone, they said. When I took off my pants, they pointed a flashlight to tickle my privates. When nothing untoward happened, they unspooled my eyes, affixed a ladder to my chest, went down inside. And when they found suitcases and saddle bags stuffed with cram books in places where they expected a heart, they wanted to go up the head, perform a CT scan. *Why this assault on my past?* In the interest of science and safety, it was their right. *You will be disappointed*, I said. But they snatched at my body, turned it over, shook it down. Suddenly on haunches, foraging the cold floor they were surprised to find in my spilled innards dark rings in the pattern of a tree trunk and deeper inside, a contraption made of lenses, wheels, buttons and a pendulum covered in blood and body fluids. When they got busy putting the pieces together and realized it was a clock—an ancient sundial on a crumbling temple yard of a forgotten civilization—doing only a circular time they had long replaced with atomic hands precise to the millisecond—they put it in the trash. *Why this travesty?* They didn't want to talk. But when someone drew up close to my face and I whispered in the singsong of lost rain-rivers how grateful I would be to be restored to the precise linearity of predictable futures, he laughed and let me off without having to repeat my name again, what was it like where I was from. *Why? Don't you want to know?* The blues were playing on the waves all this time. He yawned. He was tired of the blues.

Trout

Slur of dried rain on the glass window, shadow on the porcelain urn; a lazy afternoon spread out on the mantel crammed with trophies of war, trinkets with hidden switches to turn the lights on the fade of memory; wish magnets, quaint places peopled with storms on their faces; a round halo on the crystal Gods piled on rafters reaching a brass temple dome; dull shine on the spotless granite counter; blinding glint on the cured blade of steel running symmetrically through thyme and parsley, brinjal and bergamot, and amidst all the stagecraft of light and shade a lonely trout—mouth open—a weary pirate licking up the oozing of skin and space—a buddha reclined on a luminous chaise enjoying a sun bath caked in roasted peppers—eyes gleaming like an ancient mirror, absorbing each tiny movement in the ritual of bread. And as I looked again, the dark inchoate ring around the silver scales began to form into skin, a live halo, it started to move inside the folds, morphed into a face I had long forgotten. And the longer, I stared it started to look familiar, like my own, its beady eyes growing each minute like two headlamps converging at a distance within.

The Seemingly Irreconcilable Differences Between a Happy Poem and a Sad Poem

For a change, I wanted to write a happy poem. One that'd have no nightmares from childhood, no traces of the failures waking up at five before getting on the highway to clean up past transactions inside a gray cubicle, for bread. Not even the shadow of Ray Carver by the window watching paper boys deliver in the snow. Or Grace Paley making a pie, instead of poetry, or Bly whirling at night after accidentally touching the metal lid of a frozen mailbox. But then, what could such a poem inhabit? Sex can be happy, but not when the beer has gone flat, birds have gone quiet, and you hear tornado sirens. Not the memory of the walk back from the sacristy drunk in God-blood, grappling the darkness of woods where we lost our tongues. Maybe I'm going about it the wrong way. Maybe for a poem to be happy, rather than to add, I should be taking stuff out—like news from the world inhabited by people I no longer want to talk about, or brothers who ran away with all the beauties I conjured getting laid . . . I'd be lying if I said I don't miss the beauty of back then, I do . . . missing that makes me sad. Perhaps for a poem to be happy it's best to write up the idea of it, like a hangover. Because I can't force it, can't see it coming and when it does arrive I'm anxious about the caprice of the chance encounter, and sometimes when I head in thinking it's there, it's not—a kind of place I don't want to go today, in this happy poem.

For a change, I wanted to write a sad poem. For instance, I wanted to write about that day when alone on a bench by a creamery, on a concealed culvert, designated for those who had failed to correctly spell the names of all the stars in the closest constellation, I felt undeserving of love. But since we were in grade school, and I steadily sank into other humiliations of getting to know the history of my desires, in retrospect, it didn't seem to be the kind of profound sadness I wanted in this poem. Later, in a strange town, when I walked down the main street, outside the crêperie, a woman with a high head bun and awestruck, tooth gap—I could tell from the sweat—smelled exactly like my mother—as she rolled the crepes. When she failed to recognize me, I felt undeserving of being remembered. But since I was at work, and there were others who failed me more profoundly, it didn't seem to be the kind of sadness, I wanted in this poem. And, much later, when we were gathered on a crevasse, summer darkened around the river carrying all the silver fish and naked mermaids—clouds stand still, choking a curved sky—everyone without exception gathered in a long line, pulsing quietly like a river struck by lightning at a distance—an illusion perhaps—lasting only a few seconds before flecks of gold fanged out like rain—a real fire in a real forest—nested in plumes as if a punctured cloud had collapsed under its own weight—perhaps it was rain—but no—it was fire—and as everyone stood watching the flushed wood—not a word—no one breathing, just stoic surrender—I felt underserving of the trees. Looks like a meteor burst, someone said. That's how the dinosaurs went, someone said. But being a tiny sugar ant and hollow—the idea of somehow surviving extinction filled me with hope—not the kind of place I want to go today, in this sad poem.

The Emperor of Silk

The emperor of silk was once the emperor of dying. Since three thousand silkworms were sacrificed for every pound of silk and hundreds of pounds were woven every night in hundreds of cultures around the world, back then each silkworm had very little time. *What's the purpose? The purpose is to die*. They would sway in chorus—eyes closed, hands cupped in prayer. Their temples wrapped in sheer chiffons, gold gauzes, brocades and crepes had no other lamps, pews or mirrors.

But since the possibility of sin is endless, they had to have confessionals run by lush worms who, having failed to cocoon, were permitted to grow into butterflies.

Zhuang Zhao said, *once upon a time I dreamt I was a butterfly*. But Lao Tzu said *if you are depressed you are living in the past, if you are anxious you are living in the future.* And since the story of the silkworm dating back to the Chinese Neolithic is about surviving colonization, Lao Tzu's dream must be about the silkworm dressed like a butterfly in the afterlife.

Then they turned the page. *What's the purpose?* New pontiffs offered a different take. *The purpose is to dream.* But there were those with no faith in dreaming—the doubters and doom-mongers. *Why dream, if you have to end up a tie?* They stayed awake, burning down the fringes. But everyone knew their fires couldn't last. Because to stop dreaming is way harder than being dead.

At the Chophouse for News Addicts

At the chophouse for news addicts, it was still evening. No one at the bar but me. One more shot, I said. The barman looked me over, I am out of that stuff, he said. Go home. He was older, buffed, golden-haired, square-jawed, ready to laugh at anything I said, or to weep, when I told him about the string of unfortunate accidents that brought me to him, eyes like blue brindle. His perfume was haunting me, but he held me down with his tongue. Just one more shot I said, hoping for a different answer. No more tonight. I am closed, he said. There's something wrong with the fix, I said. Why don't I feel it yet? Come back tomorrow, he said. I have stronger stuff back in the cellar. My hands shook as I tried writing a cheque. I staggered, made one false step after another, trying to lift my body, balance my feet, walk the wet floor with dignity. Let me help you, he said. Out on the porch, I tripped and fell on my face by the concrete planter with bloodshot geraniums, beautiful night ants swarming around crumbs of sugar. Behind my back I could hear the shutter drawing down, lights shutting out. The shadow of the barman disappearing into night. Just one more shot, I cried out as loud as I could before I grabbed the papers folded over the planter, lighted a BIC. He stopped and turned, like a giant anteater, long tongue piercing the fog, touched me, dead cold; slimed into my eyes. Let me have them for the night, he said. Barely awake, I couldn't get him off. I can't explain the sounds my eyeballs made as he broke them down and popped them in one by one.

Minutes from the Meeting on Garden Failures at the Society of Smiths

#3 did it again. It's supposed to be Rembrandt, Darwin, Kaufmanniana, Double Ice Cream, Angelique, Fringed, Grand Perfection, Haley's Comet, Show Girl, Slawa, and Double Sun. And then, repeat. They have ruined the rhythm and are restrained for two seasons from raising tulips.

Chickweed, crabgrass, quackgrass, bindweed, lion face, creeping Charlie, nutsedge, cinquefoil, clover, pigweed, purslane, poison ivy, parsley, thistle in all 14 Calls to #4. Their garden has been seized by the Federation of Form.

#23's hydrangeas were all leaf no flower. When experts pointed at the low phosphorescence the owners said it has always leafed, never flowered, and that pushes that out of our pay grade. They have been referred to the Bureau of Repose.

14's Holly reported no berries. We found their bushes were both the same sex. We didn't want to bother or break anything and left it to the Department of Balance to bear out as befitting.

6, 8 and 10 showed off some spindly, rust-sick roses. Yes, we have had our share of wuss but to emphasize shortfall over strength is to shade into delusion. They are ordered to reseed.

How to Make a Cult

It's as easy as making curd. Anyone can do it. Other than milk the only essential tenet is mould. Milk is easy but mould is hard. Mould comes in different avatars. To grow mould in your house garden, first you trellis a frame—stakes on top of stakes—then you make arms, glue a hairpiece, prime a shirt. An old plaid shirt used to be good enough when I tried it once, back in time, but now you can try polyester or plastic if you want your cult everlasting. It's important to attract the sun in ascending order. Every origin story needs an arc. First a little light, then a little shade, followed by lots of reflection, redemption, rescue, reparation and preparation. Now, get back to the mould frame, slide the shirt through the arms, stuff it with hay if you have hay. Hay is cheap. But hay attracts mice. Mice are bad for mould. Mice are bad for cults. Mice steal rennet. Mice are always first to leave the tent. Stay away from mice. If you can manage, try to cult the curd with dried frankincense, myrrh, mint, sage, cardamom. More exotic the better. Cinnamon is potent—keeps mice out, also mosquitoes, and when inhaled deeply induces a good night's sleep and dulcet dreams. Now go back. Give the mould- frame some hands, feet, face—halfway between smile and scowl—just to plant the doubt in both, the seeker and apostate. Make sure the mouth is half open for the wind to whistle, so the mould, when it flowers, can sing with minimal effort. Flowery mould songs make you feel loved. Love songs attract dreamers and sleepers, those who believe in the bicycle of birth and rebirth. Remember, no one can be alone making cult. Remember, growing a mould can be tricky because mould is not like a regular root tree, it's a fungus with a mind that flowers: mould can't stay exposed to weather too long, almost always falls to the slightest shake shock. Make sure to secure the mould frame to something strong. Fences, walls, pillars, platforms. Find something with the height that allows everyone to look from far up to the mould flowering. Something with a post-podium and base so even when the mould-flowers do nothing it appears to be looking at the stars. Now, impart the final touch, make the mould frame look like a proper person, add shape, features, colour—plastic apples for eyes, nose with a giant plastic carrot. Rabbits love carrots. Rabbits make the best rabbit holes. You need rabbit for curd. You set curd in a warren of rabbit holes. Rabbits feel whole in a cult. But you got to be careful, the carrot on the face is a prop. The nose cannot be eaten. Make sure to move the mould frame around the yard. Keep it in bright sun because pests that feed on ripe fruit—starlings, crows, ants—they are smart. They almost always figure fake mould pretty fast. Once you have your mould, test it. Easy. Add milk to mould like tenet. Stir. Keep flame heat low. Do yourself a favour. Have faith in your milk. Season to taste.

Salmon

Out in the woods, it was late, the moon nearly full, vapid, in a vacant sky, slow dancing to the white heat that had exploded a skunk dead on the September trail along the patch leading to the river. Not too far. Slow. As if it were thinking. Or plain anxious. Pregnant with dead leaves, taking in all the heat, now the dark and the hint of rain. Not trees, but the shades of burnt earth visible in the stars and dry, their murmur unmissable, ready for fire. It was late. The terror of being found alone in a charged forest had choked me up. I might even be neither walking nor running but combusting like the love bugs sparkling up stones past lighted windows of gilt-nailed houses and golden treetops, scaring the night jars before I heard someone talking in whispers, a family of new migrants hunched on the gravel, on all fours, like a bear with sixteen limbs, four distinct heads, cloyed in the moonshine, eight eyes following every move. As I got closer, clapping wildly to keep away fireflies hovering the elflock like an elastic hairnet fitted to the shape of my head, they ignored me, back turned to the river, armed with scoop nets, plundering pregnant salmon as they drove against odds—the fish—shiny sheet steel, mindful of nets, aware of the undertow—like us, hunters and gatherers, and unlike us, reckless, as they smelled their way back to their natal waters to close a circle, return a debt, spawn in school benches where they learned their first alphabet.

In a Country Theatre

The only actor on stage fixated on a rolled carpet before belting out his unbroken line.

After you were gone   in the brass urn   the residue is your time   I thought of prayers   and true penance is being   and I do bury in my chest the good in time   and the gentle touch separated from time   waiting for that day when everything will un-matter   like ash   but it's winter out   and I can barely see that far in the dense night   but I can hear hoofbeat   sense   the winged horse now hiding in the urn now bent at a distance like a fiend driving the coulter of his plough deeper into my itinerant heart   pushing the weight of his frame against April   earth   In the dimming distance a horizon   Some day we shall split open the chest and spray the ash back to the earth where I can belong and wait for the wind and for the river to ripple   make pearl from salt   make salt from pearl and for the ash   now a shiny metal blob to come alive   now a catfish now a convulsing eel about to reveal something we couldn't have sensed that day when I hid in my trunk the gold of Agamemnon and did my best to keep the voice masked and blood slipping down my face

His delivery pocked with pauses; he looked around. After a long silence, the audience spilled to the edge of their seats, breath suspended, waiting for something more—the climax—for the farce to end in some sort of epiphany. No. Not all their journeys have ended in bathos. And when the actor went down on his knees and hugged the rolled carpet they were all sobbing for good reason.

Tithonus of Past Plagues

When the kitchen lights go out and the dishwasher dies, swarms of winged ants leap out of my chest of old photographs. They walk on wood, ceramic, carpet wool, mud gods. They hold their lines straight. Several hundred in a single file—like my own fragments from past wars—losers and lifers, duds and dorks, fools and felons, nerds and morons—my partial personas—towards a horizon lit like pull-taffy-molasses, their intractable spines curved on the licorice veneer of the mantel, transparent wings set on fire by a slice of moon. Their bloated shadows lolling like blow-up giants.

Why are they walking, someone asks. If it weren't your own voice from the past you wouldn't bother answering. And if you weren't out of mercy you won't be hoping to be forgiven. If you weren't choked out of words you won't be trying to hush down your head with another mouthful of insomnia pills. In one compulsive leap you grab the vacuum, try to blow the winged fragments out of the empty spaces now occupied in concentric picket lines. But they are shadow-immortal, the more you try to blow them out they come back harder.

And now you want to negotiate—talk to your past fragments about their wings, about the arc in their spine causing the disease with your seeing 20X20, about their future even though they are doddering and decrepit, fat with your unclaimed belongings. You want to talk about place and time—how they survive, how deep they travel the dark, how much more they need to journey inside your untraversable tunnels—no ideas, questions, ambition just instinct—one foot ahead of next—in slow motion—ponderous like a flood of sweet slush that smells like the vodka you have opened. And if you too weren't sleepless you wouldn't wait to figure how they coalesce to conclusion—why are they nocturnal—fear of predators/fear of sun—and what do they have to do with your self-pity like a fracture in the skull—guilt—like a disease of spine. To shut them out you turn on the TV.

Now the shadows are gone, there is nothing to worry, other than the fact of the knowledge they exist. And now that I have seen them—my undead armies of unresolved wars—I can't unsee. And as I turn to face the chest of photographs—I yield to their gravity—I want to return to those fragments, my alternative histories of counter factuality. I want to bore into the wood, walk with them, show up against the pull-taffy-molasses horizon like a blow-up balloon in the dark. But as I take the first steps I flounder before realizing: to walk into the licorice of your past wars you got to be fully awake. And it is then you recall Homer's hymn to Aphrodite—perhaps you're the Tithonus of your pasts—immortal so long you breathe and destined to be transformed into winged ants.

But you don't dwell on it. Because back in mythologies when Gods could show up thieves—still fertile for lab experiments, still early for elegies—it was the right climate for odes: to walking back from wars awash in glory, walking up to the scullery to steal the jaggery, to temples and museums of the soul. But now, even though the TV is loud, and the pills are doing their bit, the vodka working, the window stainless, the sky almost reachable, and winged ants from all the unfinished wars coiled around every touchable surface on your chest . . . prolonging the night. And since you are a sucker for happy endings, and since the past is not always perfect, and since an ode is also an elegy you think you're hallucinating. It's funny. You laugh. You drink. You don't sleep. You can't.

How I Learnt About Wars

1971: War is bad for children Mother would say but stories are good because when there's war the windows are to be permanently shut lights switched off everyone needs to hole up in a room down in the dungeons waiting for the bombs to stop and for the walls to stop rattling after the tanks have passed and for the guns to stop in the east of where she was born

1962: In the room even before I was born Father would say *there are no friends or brothers in war and* brothers would size themselves up against the bald eyeballs of brothers and mothers would feel their hearts beating against their daughters clung tight against a Chinese toy

1984: Soon someone would start a story to raise spirits change the subject and invariably it'd be the story of the golden child with the magic tongue whose singing could stop the fire freeze the bombs restore the men and women and children charred beyond time

1992: And then the singing would start first it'd be an old lover's blood visiting Bombay and they would sing fearlessly making room for my lover her gold-hennaed curls popping out a white headscarf and soon the dungeon would be filled with her damp Basbousa voice

2001: And as the lines of the dirge would pass like a baton from my lover to my son and his friends from preschool and back to me one era to the next from those who have seen war on the West Side Church or Liberty Street to those who have only seen it in movies and museums a strange vice would grab their throats their tongues would stir but no sound would turn up

2003: *No Not me I'm not the one with the magic tongue to staunch the thousand and one nights of Arabia* my son would shake his head and they would all stop

2012: But because all this happens in a story in an afternoon's history class the children I'm teaching Syria and we are all forever children in a forever history class we would have our tongues intact oh yes and we'd try to out-sing everyone each one convinced we are the golden boy / girl possessed with the golden tongue that'd stop the tanks freeze the bombs

2023: And the story would make us braver and prouder ready to face a real war   and because there's always a war going on somewhere in a pandemic and in the deepest winter when children have to be bundled inside masks and parkas *It's a good story* our parents would say and they'd never deny us another history class

After Deborah Harding

Aboard the Adriana

When all eyes were rivetted to a sub puncturing the ocean pit for the lost Titanic, a small, brown man, about thirty, nameless, but engulfed in light so blinding it was impossible to see, raising himself to a pulpit of plastic canisters in the pit of the Adriana, moments after it entered the Greek port of Pylos, addressed a gathering. He didn't hesitate. He knew what they needed.

Now that we are being told they see us, as the minister of our little prayer, let me say this, we who shall be counted among those who sold everything to hang on to our hunger, at least we are not fugitives of the soul. Look at this compass tattooed to my heart, look at the Ionian blue reflected in my eyes—clear forecast—how could we all be wrong? Look at my body, like the hull of countless voyages in countless seas, battered, but not broken, do I look like a victim of greed? We, the collaterals of colonists, children of root plants, forced into prisons of autocatalytic falsehoods, prisons of shrinking seed and fallow rattle, now is when we need the new forests marked, new plantations to harvest our will. Look at my hands, smothered, but not weak, look how I hold on to the hard-begotten testaments of sand. In the blinding sun, it might seem I'm standing on the edge of a knife. I might sound like a guitar, strapped on all sides with stringy metal, perhaps I could break any moment into hymns of hurt, regret. But those scarred by the sun can't be scared of hypothermia. Let me spell this out clear—over the kack kack of peregrines and the clatter of waves battering all the sides of this rusty fishing trawler—this is no ship anyone shall remember—it's our ark to another birth. Now is the time we gather our spices and salts. Go get your tongues and tools of trade, revise the enchanted yarns pulled out the corners of the eyes of those that made this passage before us. Let not my passion mislead your passion, or my desperation invoke your desperation, do only that's clear. Countless others have made this voyage countless times over many centuries before us. Some of us didn't make it. But to make our time count, is to be ready to die trying; beauty in such death is inevitable, no matter the purpose, occasion, place or time; and if we weren't meant to die from guns, pests, or germs at least we don't want to die dreaming of freedom. They say freedom is myth, don't bother them. Our heart of limestone and pepper flakes is not the heart that lost faith in glory and miracles. Despite the salt, look at me, look how the sun spreads out evenly over my wounds. We are martyrs.

After the spiel, the minister of this lost ceremony climbs up to the deck and asks to be seen. *Why don't you see us?* Snakeheads with pointed guns don't yet shoot at him. But he realizes now is not the time for rehearsals, no more room for reversals. Vultures and godwits circle the air, watch from a distance. And when the minister sees his fellow believers leaping off the starboard, pulled into the high seas, beating the ocean surf, cowering in the cold, restless for breath, disappearing without a trace, he licks at his reflection. *Don't behave like peonies, you infidels*, he shouts over the waves, to those that are yet to jump off the stern, *you should know God is all merciful, and hope survived every ocean in every history.* And when someone pushes him off-board he remains calm, before bursting into light, invisible to all.

Discarded Baguettes

Later, when I was drained looting the last of the discarded baguettes from dirty dumpsters behind the health food grocery, a voice woke me from the deep concentration it took me to arrange them according to degrees of decomposition. The voices were oozing out a place inside my eyes where a vessel had dislodged after a massive storm. It was a woman's voice. It was a man's voice. It was a river's voice—in a loopy gravelly rhythm. I knew that voice. It was demanding I return since drifting is futile and all roads converge to the rubbish heap. *But there are worms in that dirty baguette,* I said. *Stop stealing*, someone said. I ran as fast as I could. I must have been hungry. I was wounded. But to be hungry is one thing and to be cheated of a perfect baguette by your own head is quite another. And as I slept, the voices drew closer, not like a dream, but out of the sticky bubble goo on the mirror, stretched out like snakeskin. I looked inside, realized the mirror was no longer reflecting images but voices oozing out my own belly button—rising and falling like breath—reeking garlic butter which I had spread evenly onto each baguette before I devoured them one by one according to degrees of decomposition, keeping the best for last. *What has happened to you? How could you do it? Come back now . . .* The mirror repeated like a drumbeat.

At a Gathering for Long Life

At a gathering for long life salt-crusted salmon was being baked with blood orange, pasta boiled in the blood of oysters. *What colour is oyster blood*, someone asked. Outside, geese with black heads cackled as they dodged contrails from fighter jets, birches with peeled skin stood vigil like rigid anglers in bucket hats reeling in the sun. When the sun slipped in a pool of blood everyone got back in and started beating the wet breeze with Japanese sensu before stopping to examine the shadow box with pinned butterflies and cut asters floating on bubble rafts. Someone stood up and started clinking glass to drown out the crickets soldering rivets into the night. She was wearing a blue wig, blue lip gloss, blue contact lenses over brown eyes. *The secret to long life boils down to a purple potato*, she said. Apparently, no one had seen a purple potato before. Someone raised her hand, in sotto, *why not the golden potato? What about the bitter gourd,* someone spat out acid cheese, *grown in boxes in my back garden. Fuck potato. May all die exactly like we are today*, the host raised a toast, before some disbelieving pagan drew his puckers and shot at a dartboard missing him by centimetres. After a game of wink murder, everyone went silent before someone strummed on a guitar interrupted by someone else who wanted to talk about the design of a slaughterhouse—chute with hairpin curves, solid walls, no shadows, hushed whispers in the area where sheep are stunned. *I am sick of being sold short*, someone said. *Let's do it*, someone held up a piece of papaya while removing corn with the tip of his tongue. *Let's never die*, someone said searching his pocket for eyeglasses. *Amen,* everyone said, before standing up to savagely swat at bees that had somehow breached an outer wall, broke into the vent, crashed the party.

still life broken

is like that mobius strip the loop is not endless but I won't count bulbs in the bathroom because she likes it dark nor hinges on those doors after years of shut slamming for no reason or sun as it creeps silently the lost child between shadows of strip-naked tamarack walking alone after a hit a long hit out in the dark when no one is looking everyone asleep he stands by the wall in pieces seamed together with a dark thread or just darkness mistaken for thread like the lightly writhen body of the crystal wine jug from unknown antiquity heritage fate put together with light mistaken for glue like words between pauses sewn up with spit semen breath something concrete colourless palpable like faces we know firsthand broken on one side held in place by physics and we know because we have been practicing taking apart putting back again like blocks of a Japanese pillow book hidden behind the closet

Gladiators

In the City Hall, after the dog show, two old men started a fight. Strangers in ripped jeans and cactus squeezed into the aisles egging them on. They seemed like old friends dressed like gladiators, locked in wraps of leather, old iron. *You are a radical fart* said the one with oval glasses. *You're a square turd* said the one with brow lines. Waving their walking sticks like sabres they repeated ancient slurs over and over: *you blood-sucking pumpkin*; *you louse-infested poppycock; you stinky manure heap; you blathering balloon of burps; you low-life sea snail; you filthy fiddlestick.* Soon they were shaking each other by the throat, belching anguished gasps into each other's eyes flush with tears to make up for the loss of words from half Nelsons. The crowd stood on the edge of time waiting for the turning point; something more extreme. They were already bored. They had seen a million gladiators before. So, the wigs came off, then the glasses. After a short headlock, they were crawling the length of the hall's cracked floor looking for their teeth. *Help me find my eyes you scumbags* one said, head cocked towards the raucous mob. *Help me find my clothes you bastards* said the other. No one in the pews moved. No one knew if they were real or ghosts, history dressed up for the evening news.

Ants Want to Remember

After the hard summer when trees cast off their skin and academies of the underworld reopen to train the fallen in the art of death, sugar ants careen down tunnels bored with their tongues, watch their long shadows on the oblique sun, hunger to be kissed and touched. Later, the tangled arms of the birches take over the body of the yard like a looming—not just a metaphor of deep or freeze—a state of time, moving slowly, like wet shadows on snow, heaving footprints. Then there's spring. And we are returned to Ms P's delphinium across the street and Ms Q's daffodils at the turn, and Ms R's Lenten rose by the trail, and meadow rues by the river, adonis and tulips, squills and hyacinths that grow without prompting or purpose in the wasted yard of alliums around upright headstones. In the cemetery, we don't talk about the frenzied wind blowing dirt into the cursive chiselled on granite and peonies in plastic containers. We sit on an iron bench, watch the river, listen to the cackle of geese billowing in the folds of the ravine, half-taken by mist before it gets too dark for children to be out safe. When the sun slips away we want to be remembered, so we pose in the golden light keeping a third dark, two-thirds open to possibilities; for immortality, we get a piece of the red-winged blackbird circling the great heron mining silver in the stippled glass.

Pyramids in Purgatory

Since primary school I have chased pyramids—their triangular eyebrows perfunctorily pasted on timepieces, travel brochures, and TV. I have imagined Pharaohs permeated in afterlife meta morphing into gods. Out the window, the sun is desert yellow. And since I was permitted to hold sugar in my crock, I have wondered how far up the brickwork lime must one crawl to be among Pharaohs and gods glowing like lighted coal on the capstone covered in gold-plated tendril arabesque, reflecting the skies. Pharaohs are well preserved, gods are luminous, and I am in a skin bag needing sugar. But it's not impossible to look at the crystal ball and imagine, believe even, further up, beyond the azure tessellations, there's hidden another cluster of pyramids, another hierarchy of gods and Pharaohs—a new set of triangles and trinities—overlapping and interlocked—cold, like faces on a morning commute, lush like amaryllis blowing out of tender bulbs. You can feel they are at a distance. And you are not the one with vertigo, you don't believe the high road to heaven is just hot air—empty trumpets floating above the tarpit—you believe in cause and effect. You are the obedient square in a room of four clerestory splits—happy when they explain the soul as meaningful refraction, but when you look for the amaryllis and it's gone there comes a moment when the pyramids powder down into sand and it feels as if dreams are just dirt—one moment you were dipping into marmalade, licking the tits of paradises lost, next moment feeling the tongues of ghosts around the collar bone, maelstroms moving in circles inside your throat. Then you feel you have been cheated since you were thirteen. Down below, in the folds of a dirt pit, you know there are lovers and friends that fell off the ledge last night, fending off shadows, foraging rotten apples, ruined pomegranates; you don't hear them, but you know, not because of the fear of labyrinths—because you were born in the dirt pit; because you don't want to revisit that tenderloin of fallen ants—and when someone among the fallen sticks up wings around their spiracles and preen at the high mirror pretending to fly, you don't notice because failure violates you—pushes you to that place between promise and perdition—the sterile pyramid-purgatory you earned—where doors up the stairs close the moment you enter.

In the Big Basin Redwoods

It was a carnival of masks. We were all dressed up in coloured feathers, fancy hair pieces—walking along the ash aftermath, ghost remnants, watching spiders furrowed in the tanned bark. To reclaim our ghosted souls, we painted bright pictures, lay on the scarred ground pretending to stop the ghost train that could only be heard; glued our wing pits to the tar, entered the epicormic centre of immortality—now dark and empty—pressed our ears to the other forest underground, sentient for centuries, now stunned by lightning. When the wind stopped, we realized there were no birds—dense gloomy silence overcast like a cloud, dark tunnels hung like blisters on the bark, waiting for rain—we started singing. It was a carnival of masks; the creek like a water drum could only be heard. *What kind of bird are you*, someone asked. *Do you do rivers and roses or just the burning infernos? Failed love? Fallen heroes? Roses nauseate me*, I said. *Why are you here? What did you lose? What do you have to repent for? Are you attracted to nothing but darkness?* Before I could answer, someone pushed me from behind. *If you have nothing to own is there anything you can ever find? What about the past, I said.* No one had time, no one waited to see where I fell. *You aren't real. You are made of empty words. We can't even touch you*. I could hear the echoes ringing. Not tongue-tied; just awestruck; the redwood was alive and present. *I am glad you even saw me*, I said. But they seemed to not hear; perhaps they had lost their tongues, perhaps they were in a hurry to get back to wherever they came from. It wasn't yet night, just a carnival of masks, drums at a distance. The trees seemed tired of projections. They wanted to be alone. They didn't want birds.

Boy With a Short-Tailed Diamond

A friend from childhood shares a picture from back when I was eight or nine, flying a short-tailed diamond in a bright shirt with stars, on the border of a drain-river back home, half buried in waste oozing from the lungs of algae-green houses lined on the right. On the left, a clump of blackboard trees. Like a bushy sideburn tin rooftops shine in a haze of aged photo paper. The sky—a distance away—is luminous, dazzling, incandescent—pocked with other long and short diamonds—not the usual grey I remember dreaming up later. Closer ground, empty spaces surrounding the boy fill up with a version of my own face now, several decades later, a man's face—angled to the left—the flagellating drain-river shaped like a nose, a clump of scaly houses filled with cracks like the dry lips reflected on the plastic mirror. Windows of two drowning houses from back then, like eyes so dark you don't look for fear of getting sucked into it. Those are my eyes now. And those eyes are dangerous. Hollow with shock, burnt electric sockets, they reflect someone else. No longer the boy from childhood with a tailed diamond in the sky. It's a face weakened by long travels, unending wars, warts and lumps and other obvious deformities of time. This man who fills up the emptiness around his own childhood is also smiling and that's a causal coincidence. The smile of that much-travelled man is schmaltzy but not regretful, wry but wistful. He seems to be smiling at the distance he travelled and also at the devastation of the place he started from. His most recent acquests limned on the lighted computer screen against the ruins of his origin. It's that kind of smile—hungry and hunting beauty in the past, presently desperate for redemption. But the boy in the bright shirt with stars on the edge of the drain-river is oblivious of futures. He's no illusion or accident. He's real. He isn't there to impale a cloud and drench himself in the rain of ancient wisdom even though he's looking upwards. He's there to drag his glass-smeared manja down the throat of the other diamond kite threatening to kill him. Looking at the two—the shadow of the man looking at the boy from childhood and the boy left behind in childhood oblivious of his eventual fadeaway—you are bound to look again not at the man who's wasted or the boy wasting with so much beauty but at the meaning of it all. What of beauty then if the sky that holds all our faces in time-tangled-arcs reveals all its truths at once? What of distances that look beautiful in time and become grotesque inside a reflection? When that occurs, what happens to all the beauty in the child frozen in that place? If beauty in that photo from childhood is merely a concoction, why is the boy with a tailed diamond still smiling at the man who travelled far?

Jasper 2024

Everyone has seen it by now. The still-standing spire of a church on the corners of Geikie Street & Miette Ave, caught in fire. It started in 1913 out of a small box car and dry logs of cedar donated by the McCalls of the Grand Trunk Pacific Railway. The red episcopal door, the ancient vestibule holding holy water, aisles of wood; altar and choir and the chancel deep into the narthex of nonbelievers, the nave and the cubbies of cedar, the vestments and the Red Books of Prayer, all gone. No one to kneel today or taste the Eucharistic blood—no robes or records in the broken sacristy. Yet the stone walls covered in soot, foregrounding tall pines stand in a clear blue haze of the mountain fog and the marquee, bleary in the smoke from embers still lifting off the yard, points at the two black spruce dugs foregrounded in memory like shot holes, sucking chest wounds.

The wound of the burnt tree shrouded in the smoke of the burnt church takes time to settle, yet so many trees—since they appeared three hundred sixty million years ago—have quietly given their lives for so many churches, temples and inner cities. And yet, it is the chest wound of the cedars that fill so much of Jasper that survive outside photo cups of memory doused in sorrel and saxifrage, spruce, aspen, pine and birch, moss in shapes of anemone, avens and forget me nots. Just like a fire mark, a gun wound defines the body.

And what else does a bullet do? It shatters the brain, cooks blood from burgundy to chocolate, thick enough to coat the back of a wooden spoon. An expanding clot takes over tissue, forms into failure. And what is failure? Beyond forfeiture of the laws of earth, fire, and water where twice stepped, no one is ever the same, failure is a start. And a forest twice born is like a reincarnated God, like Grizzly 222 who survived this Jasper and yet was reborn. And the bear on Patricia

Street, built by James Simpkins in 1948, lodged in the brain like a piece of confetti that never stops calling.

What survives all fires is our inheritance—time travelling at twisted speeds, witness testimonies of life in different places defying the gravity of memories locked in black cottonwood and silky phacelia, avens and hummingbird—muted and receding into etchings like shot wounds blending into the tissue of skin, like chocolate hope, garnished with black sesame in a cup of blood custard.

The Straight Road

After mist the dirt road tears a bed of wild roses in half. What you want is what you want. When the day is pitch dark and the dirt is a diamondback flicking its tongue, it's not the banter rising up the factory floor, nor missives of Mephisto handed to Faust.

Chi Chi Chi, when the animal jaws are taut in the hard wind, when the wild rattles and the radio is rife with theories of imminent uselessness, it's not about your fear of obsolescence; you're hungry right now. What you want is what you want: to eat freedom you need a different tongue.

To make a deal with devil you need another stomach. To love the way you want, you need rain. After rain, a blazing sun—you don't want cream, towels from Turkmenistan, you want to burn. And after roses are slaughtered in the wind, you want a rainbow. What you want is what you want.

Horses play in the barn, dragons smoke. You want to be like leaves—dead-green-yellow-red—to be no more faceless in that virus of constricted heart, to stand like a guitar, like a winter rose that has lost its fear of frost. What you want is what you want.

At a distance, the diamondback is pocked with prints, tire treads, pebbles, pollen. It rears up to meet you blind, without promises, periods, appellations as though you were bird. You want to love; you don't want to be bird. Not the sky, to plant feet on dirt. Take root. Become a tree. Shed leaves. Survive lightning. What you want is what you want.

The road is straight; you travel the straight road even though you're pregnant with volcanoes. You want to remember you're not the only one with a piercing in the tongue. It's the straight road. It's not the straight. What you want is what you want.

The Lamp of Diogenes

Jacques said there are seven ages of man in the midsummer night. But if death is the caesura for another cycle of seeking and being the forever alien is a long tunnel and if the breaks in line are decided by programmers in Redmond, the history of time is just false prose. If it's suffering we are after, between cycles of crumbling, should we dunk our face in ether or hurt? Should we listen to the twitter of the starling or the silence in between? Do we remain unmoved because we are no longer pristine, not full of promise and yet not utterly undamaged? Do we live in hope for a new cinder, or do we break clean when we finish, re-alloy after every dying as amber or a dead knife?

After taking in the questions Diogenes lit the lamp and started looking.

In the seven stages of the soul, first, you conjure the dream. Keep hair wet before running the comb. You don't have to disagree with the dark night. I speak from deep familiarity, he said. *Don't resist what you don't know. Keep nothing in memory. Hold firm, candle to face, don't avert eyes. Keep gestures like river-worn stone, make words discard clothes, make sense as if you were straddling spirits. Know the doors. There's nothing to feel when you are in laughter. After all the lively striving, exhausted, you are so put together to take on what's not coming.*

Long after the projector stopped, the few that outstayed its friendly murmur, huddled over pea soup and country bread, chatting up the actors before carrying the lanterns to the bar. Good night, someone said before leaving. Good night. Good night, everyone repeated.

Where Are You From Where Are You Going

My father said, to escape questions of origin is to escape your mother. To escape your mother—when she is asleep, long after the day broke, wounded after the long night's brawl in the dirty old tavern—is to be the forever fugitive, eyes compounded like ants, ears cut up in catacombs, incapable of sensing movements of your feet.

My mother said, to escape questions of origin is to escape your father. To escape your father is to escape the knotted blood and to escape knotted blood is to be forever bleeding into your own shadow like dead rivers, sunk mountain passes, silkworms feeding on mulberry before being baked into pyjamas, comforters and sleeping bags.

My lover said, to escape questions of origin is to escape being naked. To escape being naked is to escape the fugue. To escape the fugue is to become the cicada—emerging out of tunnels every 13-17 years for a lengthy reconnaissance of losses: forfeitures of memory, sense of proprioception, sudden closures of arteries, broken hands of clocks.

Things To Do When You Get Home

When you follow the flavours of cumin and cardamom, you don't doubt your senses, you don't doubt the nature of the devil's tree. You don't doubt the soul presiding over dead roosters on grills oiled with peanuts and seasoned with the seeds of charlock or sesame. When you follow the arc lights back into the country and in the dim skylight your shadows from the near and distant pasts trail you like lost sheep, in that shadow, you don't mistake the hairpin turns, switchbacks and bends with the cesspit of Gomorrah. When you follow the songs that never abandoned you and watch yourself in the mirror, you are amazed, as the tongue, dry like an unused interval splits in two, along the grain of muscle, and quickly treated with ointments of ingenuity, releases morphemes of claim and inheritance. When you get off the sidewalk and scale the mighty stoop facing the wood door you touch in your dreams daily, your legs fail because you are still fugitive, you own nothing and when you search for a meander to loop back in time no one can understand your urgency. And you can't tell them about the lost sheep, lost sleep, lost feet. You have no language either.

A Wound is a Potato

If a seed goes into the ground and dies it will grow, Christ said. You wait for spring, dig dirt, bury the seed deep. Now you are worried about rabbits, pests, fungi, Gods. But it's in nature that the mother shall survive invasions, shoot up to inflorescence, dream in purple. But the purple potato blossom is a flower, not a wound. It can't be eaten. Meanwhile, below the ground, the mother has multiplied. Each new potato: a new wound that can be eaten. Or driven back to ground for fresh tubers to make millions of potato wounds and pollen-laden purple flowers. But what about the original mother? That mother is old and wrinkled. That mother can barely stand inside her skin. That mother can't remember how it all started. And the mother who has forgotten the wound is no longer a potato. She's just the mother who started all wounds. And no mother can be eaten.

Now Let Me Forget

what's memory but a showboat   bifocal   because you
can see both ends
boat and bile—boat in bile   float   and the slow rock and
the big horn   goodbye goodbye goodbye

show me a melody   a memorial song that
doesn't melt down the Jello drama on the highway to
billabong   "what's the song   what's the song
once more once more once more   I can't recall"   one
chance one empty

billboards screaming—"look at me" "look at me" "look at
me"   wink slow
or show the back of tongue touching the lisp wick slow tongue slow
burn sometimes   lips of a story this slow lisp story of a burn   one
burn   one time   zero recall   touching
the billet of the chest—

big cave   big bang   bang bored   throat sored kill
hoard   kill bang   will board horro' story   zero recall and
repent and lament and failure to recall things that failed

things don't matter   things that kill will   big broad bilge board and
leave   leave   leave

what? melo kiss Missy Sauga   Big Lord Big Boy billion reasons to
say goodbye goodbye to you a'l—

I liked the song   as long   all along—"you
hear me"   now let me forget.

Not Everyone Is Gone

After much effort, she pulls a dusty pouch out of a forgotten drawer and lays it out on a sheet—tan as sand—faces smudged with thumbprints—ripped in the corners. The room smells like formaldehyde. The hand-wound clock disturbs the pale white sun. By the time she walks over to the balcony, nearly everyone is gone. She doesn't have to say it. Out on the street: two boys—whose names she makes up like characters of a half-told story—balancing discarded bike tires with batons, choose a path carefully between debris and dog droppings. The sheer curtain behind her dazzles briefly before everything darkens a shade. The sun can only go so far. She worries about depleted moth balls in old sweaters before waving at Socrates out by the deli offering a discourse while stringing a dark brown harp. And then she tries to sing over a song from her childhood piping out the dirt-dimmed neon of the music shop. Someone passes by, picking used plastic bottles, licking on an ice ball. Someone sits on a spotted horse ahead of a band of shiny uniforms pouring oil into tired saxophones. A circus monkey sits chained to a tin bucket by a boy with a balance pole in a moment of inertia. She strains to read the graffiti on a stalled tram car—dark wings spread over dark treetops. Not everyone is gone, she repeats, thumbing through an old phonebook, beside an embroidery frame draped in a bright red doily, frilled with green silk tassels, unfinished under brass wing nuts.

The Denouement

We die when the brain stops remembering failures of memory. And we know it's a different kind of dying when the heart stops responding to the cackle of geese in blue mountain mist. And yet another kind when we are in a gathering, and no one remembers our name. And we die tied to a bed of aster in a country theatre and in the kettle of hope boiling a desert and shot like a duck poking out of picket fences. And like the rose, one petal at a time, not dying at all, cheated of death's final hip shake. And like the novel, periodically, when the presaged arc of our particular epic plotted so meticulously to end in something profound is quietly punctured before the action climaxes to any puissant resolution. And we die after the nightstand that no one knows how to bring back to life after the manufacturer stopped making the brand. And like a sugar ant carrying furniture fifty times our weight, so consumed by commuting to and back from the Queen's station terminus we make it our cause to pervert the presaged ending, even if that means we end up sounding like a drip drum and floating like a plastic lotus in a vapid vase. And we die climbing up and down a step ladder stood up against the chest, searching for gods, for soul, for our itinerant heart-voice. And we die in embarrassment walking back into fragments of our understanding of ourselves, skinny dip into the dead pool inhabited by our own shadows that move like serpents and morph into beavers making dams for a future that may never come. And we know that. And yet we die cutting through our own flesh and bones that we ourselves have polished punctiliously with expensive creams and fortified with vitamin milk. And we die going down deeper, past the whirlpool of shadows into our rare earth—into the bed of cobalt and nickel stuck to the fishbones of our past—and we die in a forest of kelp in a soundless tree-cave reflecting a trapped sun. And there we stop and realize we are not yet dead; we are here, still breathing.

Societies of Snow

In a yard cratered dead centre down smooth moonstone, an older man pulls at a plastic pip crouching over a patch of yellow. A boy brushes snow off a frozen machine precisely poking at holes between the engine and other parts of purpose. The man grabs a wooden shovel and faces the mountains, on both sides of neighbouring yards, clean as steel. Then the man stabs the edge of the ground near his feet, bends his knees in a posture of prayer, tosses the dead weight over the walls of this new Church grown around him suddenly, like a parenthesis. To free himself from the weight piled on the steel of his blade he must use his spine like a bulwark, but the tip of the white cupola is at a plane higher, and his bent shoulder can curve only so much. As the boy walks back he turns around and winces every time the blade breaks free from its chained Promethean shadow with a thump and the wet snow hits the pinnacle, comes rolling down the spine back to where it was—congealed like a clump of empty words. No one says a thing. No words can describe what the man is doing. Snow is prayer. Love is gesture. The boy digs into a sack and sprinkles salt before lifting his head to observe newly arrived renters in dark overcoats trudging knee deep in a singular file, busy like ants, looking for ways to pry open a frozen side door.

Of Yellow Mountains and Burnt Sequoias

After the last visitor leaves, moments before curtains are drawn, in the mirrored walls of a dim anteroom, you feel sweat breaking down your creased forehead, skin cold to touch. Rain is on its way—you can tell from the damp around your pits. A cloud has burst outside, you hear it. Perhaps the cars are about to float up like crowfoot buttercups, or hyacinth—you are not sure—whatever happens, it's still a dream like the one last night when you were lost in the canyon digging the dirty gold. You can feel your hands—dead sore. Of course, doctors have said what they had to—eventually it's always a failure of the heart to stay up with the soul. You don't visit the soul. But today you feel you have the powers to summon it at will—a snap of fingers—there it is—the djinn pointed at your head like a pole of a shadow mirror projecting you—clouded in many arguments: about the colour of a dismembered rainbow—poison in the seeds of a half eaten apple core tanning on a tray—yellow mountains along the highway from LA to San Franciso—they come rushing—like the children when you returned home after long intermezzos—they are all here—every note and interval—everything silent except the clock—everything lighted except the mirror—the animal that has invaded your lung—the sand that has invaded the webbing of your feet—the smell of waves in your breath—the aftertaste of vomit—medical alcohol. You have a vague sense of the gurney—your heart, still turning—you are no longer nervous even though you have been kept on hold. Today the police sirens don't bother you as much as the window you failed to fix—creaking up hell—and the grass you failed to cut—dancing waist high through the broken glass—wet washings like empty ghosts. You can see water climb the wall like a blurred panto. Everything drowning in the expanding siren—near past hazed out at a distance—future flashing like the little red button on the door, recording everything. What is the sense of it all? Perhaps the weight of all the words that touched you; burn in the hearts of all you touched; like the burn in your veins now. How much burn is that? A forest of charred sequoias. And how much do sequoias weigh after ashening? And what good is ash, after the curtains close? One more breath. Ah! But sequoias have immortal roots—you think—no—you know—you feel you know, before you feel—tired—no more—nothing.

The Oath

A door opens; a judge arrives; a clerk reads from a note. *Now raise your right hand. If you get disconnected, stand by*. It's that time: spring and hour for the oath. Outside, *Pest Patrol* climbs up a ladder. Beyond the window, a virus seethes. *First in English then in French.* This oath is arrival.

I swear that I will be faithful, And what's my faith: to be fulfilled in the marinade of platonic cave shadows; to cut the head, hold it with both hands, be happy; to carve the chest like a pumpkin and launch like a paraglider—the remit of origin; remand of journeys home; away; a warren of tunnels; a command failure; a float for forecasts. Skies are overcast; eaves in thaw; maybe rain; or snow. On the monitor, images pull into a pixelated mirror. This oath is arrival. This mirror is a rival. Outside, *Pest Patrol* look for holes, droppings; someone has been invading my landlady's dreams.

There she is—in her red coat, red snow boots, toque and pole strap on the red brick driveway, a colonial with a turret clock and a weather cock in a pile of snow—everything under, equal, except the birch roof—smoking. And there, her dog wants to chase the wind. No. She won't have it—ants have settled into her creams . . . Dog in the dead wind, hogging the headwind . . . Ants everywhere, she says. And she can do nothing. The walls have cracks, doors don't shut, windows grate to the slightest wind shift. Once inside, the ants dig into the apples, move like a train of manic, awestruck eyes. So small, I can't vac them out, she says. She has to bore the core down to the bottom, stain the bodies floating on milk and marmalade and just when she puts it away—hoping—dead ants are dead—ready to slice the cheese, sip on the wine, they come back to join a swarm cutting in through floorboards, cracks in the foundation. Fall is when you fasten things gone wrong in the attic, she says, but I'm late this year. Very late. I like spring, I say, the slowness more than snow-ness. And the dog is quick even in harness. And I'm synching lips to an oath at a mirror reflecting darkness.

Once, before winter, I had seen my landlady chase after aliens plundering pregnant salmon. Once, before summer I saw her cradling a nest of robins tangled in wind-snapped elm. Once, off trail, feeding deer alfalfa. She says winter is a revival. I say nothing. But we agree on eggnog; mumming masks; even when I don't always understand *And bear true allegiance To Her Majesty* who hauls me over to old lands, old wounds. Past worries her. Ant slurries her. Snow gives her hope. Sugar traps me. Wounds make me. Past has taken me. I'm good for nothing anymore. And they know, as they opened me on arrival. And in the hollow, the oath is loath, and hope is the rope to hang a pie.

Once we walked on a dead river, swapping stories about lost mothers. I said: my mother forgot me the day I left her—and now she breaks down the monitor. Mirror is failure; compass is saviour, why look back, she said. Yet when we reached the cemetery, she stopped by her husband's headstone and cleaned the snow with bare hands until she could see her face on the ledger. And when I offered my hands, she said, she needed to clean her mess alone. It was late. Sun had left a bloody pool, a speckled moon, pale as her wintered lips; at a distance, ice lit up like a drawn-out candelabra . . . and whumpf her dog in the dead wind hogging the headwind . . . Tree branches in the red fluorescent air looked like limbs of discarded clothes in my mother's dark room, always on camera. And in all the walls of my mother's room—in the warren of tunnels and train of arrivals, she hung like a mirror. And my mother, even though she has forgotten me, leans out the balcony, I'm told, to shout at strangers—*Queen Elizabeth the Second, Queen of Canada—you have mooched me*. And here, when the sky blanched out, and there were no more strangers, my landlady went back to her chair by her husband's headstone; mumbling strange morphemes that sounded like oath and prayer.

And what is your prayer? Prayer is the layer between the here and there, my landlady said, once she was done placing her flowers—an arrangement of poinsettias and holly. To pray is to cast the runes in the playroom, to oath is to play the past in the mudroom. Once, walking on the edge of the river, she said, her mother morphed into a fairy the day after she left school. And at school when we rifled failures it became clear; our histories are one long river of ferry arrivals. And even though oath is arrival and the mirror is a river—even back in time—the rivers were always dying. To trade beginnings for endings is the way of the river, she said, and the river is a beaver, and the mirror is a cleaver. Forget it. Because it's futile ferreting out frozen roots in December; forking out connections between forfeitures and forefathers. Here, take some cream, moisturize. Elsewhere is a dead river in a dream. Here, take the compass. Pasteurize lost mothers in prayer and purpose. In the cemetery, even in December, sugar ants surrounded the Queen and *Her Heirs and Successors.*

Despite the stench of death, she felt fine, she said. But I felt like I was intruding on those tombs of frozen ancestors. And I understand what it means to lose your stand after take-off, she said, but to lose your feet where you end off, hoping to be saved or acknowledged is a turn-off. Recollection of losses is whiplash, an after-crash-aftertaste. Get over it. And now, here is the thing, she said, I'm not afraid of the dark, just tired of turning. And these rivers don't just turn and die. They go elsewhere. Deep into secret runnels to refill and revive. So, death is a revival, and oath is arrival.

And the soul? What about it, she said. Don't go there, her voice rising a pitch as the river cracked into a howl under our feet. She slid her hands in mine. We slid into deathly silence, shared a joint. The call of night birds mixed with cries of children playing in a deep ravine filled us with hope. She turned, shot me a stare, gave me her apple. Eat it. My tongue frozen, my head stoned, hands dirty. I wasn't ready. I could barely move. It was cold.

No quarrel, just numb, I don't know what she thought. We never came back to that place. For long we couldn't speak. Even though we felt, whatever we felt, I knew. I lost my tongue to mirrors hanging on a wall, she lost her apples to the ant. In our failure and lack we were equal. *And that I will faithfully observe the laws of Canada* we are equal in the sequel. And now, that we survive the plague we are equal. And that we fall into a warren of tunnels we are unequal. And in the posthumous postmodern unequal. We are unequal in revival and equal in the atrophy of arrivals.

To quieten her nerves, I told her about this dream I once had: alone in the arrival hall, by the storm door, I'm waiting for someone to let me in, they put me on a gurney, cut me up, start questioning all my past pregnancies, people I'm still carrying inside. When they try sewing me back, they can't. And now this oath can't fill the wounds that festered. And outside, while she is talking to *Pest Patrol* about holes in the attic, gaps in floors and doors, she's looking at me. And now that her breath fogs the window, it feels we are like star-crossed lovers caught in a shared conveyance of lack and fail, complicit in a continuum . . . *Including the Constitution* . . . alone, in our warren of tunnels, alone in the maw of mirrors, scared of emptiness, impotence, irrelevance. Alone . . . Are we not? She said nothing. Maybe this mirror is arrival. And this oath is arrival because of the mirror.

A different kind of arrival, she said once. Because when you kill the mother who forgot you, by default you are born again. But how? With carved chest, dehiscent wounds? And in that new place in the continuum—she carried on—death is survival, failure is arrival, and guilt is a patch quilt in the deep freeze of December, driving sideways into cracked mirrors. And when you weave the oath in arrivals: *which recognizes and affirms* a new beginning . . . you are choosing to believe. And when you believe you are in faith, and you haven't failed, you haven't lost a thing, you are equal in chaos and folly, in the dark and in oath and death absolutely . . . absolutely.

What if faith is bait? Now I'm afraid. Because outside the window they are still haggling over holes, pointing at me. And now this oath is a figure. This mirror is a trigger. And bad is good and failures are failed ears, everything a parody and paradox and words are useless when you can't go out and tell her: you freeze before you eat because history is an echo chamber, guilt is a price of passage and when you give up your tongue on arrival you dig into ice with bare hands, pluck dead leaves from past summers and hope there is torque in purpose. Yes. Hope is the map and compass, she says. *Which recognizes and affirms the Aboriginal and treaty rights of First Nations, Inuit and Métis peoples . . .* I mean what else, but hope could make the ant so dead all winter, yet so ready for spring, look, how their legs are loaded fifty times their weight, if they were bird they'd be osprey.

No. Starlings maybe, she said, thought a second. Look how they troop around bus stands with backs packed with elsewhere and after world—theirs's a distinct style of murmuration—their angst never rising above the tumult of traffic, sometimes they cook overhead toying with electricity between their toes, waiting for thunder, sometimes they freeze after taking it all—seed and sugar—between their legs, waiting for the Queen. Sometimes they whistle all night. Brave and tame, meek and restless, their passage, presage, progress, contradictions are like an equation no one can solve. Even though they occupy squares their eyes move in circles. And when they nest inside basements they carry their fetor. And when they hang down windows they carry their tongues. And when they roost in attics, their silence is like the eerie no-mind, Inception top.

And now, outside the red clock house, *Pest Patrol* is sucking air out, sealing all windows. Why? Who's to ask? She's still looking at me as if it's me digging into her creams. Not at all. Besides, it's Monday. And I paid my rent last Tuesday, took the trash out before I sat for Oath . . . the oath that's arrival on the mirror that's the river flowing into the tunnel that's the trigger of wounds and failures and the compass that's the schlong of settlers and hope that's a tunnel howl and fate that's a funnel ghoul and the lust to be found and savoured and remembered the mole in the barnyard and hole in the sick heart whose sole purpose is to posthumously perpetuate a pathology of guilt and forgetting and to fail is to be equal so long I don't fail to be equal *And fulfil my duties as a Canadian citizen* and that is to mean the dog in the dead wind is the hog in the headwind and oath is survival even though the mirror is a rival and the compass is rumpus even though the clock is where we stand. We stand on the clock. And now the clerk stops. The judge would like you to place your right hand on your heart. Please stand . . . *O Canada, we stand. O Canada, we stand.*

Acknowledgements

Thanks to the Ontario Arts Council and the Writers Union of Canada for their generous grants that made this book possible. Thanks to the editors of the journals below where early versions of some of the poems appeared. Thanks to Hoa Nguyen, whose early encouragement and advice on the manuscript helped shape it. Thanks to Chantel Lavoie for her generosity and for giving this work the privilege of her time and attention whenever I reached out. Thanks to M. G. Vassanji for his careful reading and insightful edits. Thanks to Nurjehan Aziz and the entire team at Mawenzi Press for their incredible work in producing this book. Thanks to Rishi and Keka, my staunchest allies and fiercest critics, without their help, I'd be long lost foraging the castle for sugar.

Arc Poetry Magazine: "Boy with a Tailed Diamond";

The Antigonish Review: "still life broken" and "Minutes from the Meeting of the Committee of Garden Failures";

Beyond Words Magazine: "A Happy Poem";

Contemporary Verse 2: "The Art of Tea", "Seabass";

The Dalhousie Review: "Once I Boarded the Spice Train";

Diagram: "As a Sugar Ant You Are Entitled", "On a Leaf The Ants";

Nashwaak Review: "On the Commute to Work", "Street Play About a White Flower", "In The Country Sanatorium", "Studies of Wound Under a Flashlight", "Things They Do To You At The Airport", "Discarded Baguettes";

PRISM international: "The Denouement";

Rat's Ass Review: "The Fix";

Ricepaper Magazine: "Models of Migration";

Touch the Donkey: "In The Country School", "In a Country Theatre", "The Lamp of Diogenes", "Things to do When You Get Home";

WILDSound: "The Big Fight".

SABYASACHI (SACHI) NAG is the author of *Hands Like Trees* (fiction; Ronsdale Press, 2023) and three previous collections of poetry, including *Uncharted* (Mansfield Press, 2021). His work has been published in numerous journals worldwide. He holds an MFA in fiction from the University of British Columbia and is an alumnus of the Iowa Writers' Workshop, Simon Fraser University, and Humber School for Writers. He is the managing editor at *Artisanal Writer*, an online journal that explores books, lit craft, and theory. When he's not reading or teaching Creative Writing, he enjoys going paddling with his wife and son in the Great Lakes near Toronto.